Afghanistan

AFGHANISTAN
Key to a Continent

John C. Griffiths

Westview Press / Boulder, Colorado

Copyright © 1981 by John C. Griffiths

Published in 1981 in the United States of America by
  Westview Press, Inc.
  5500 Central Avenue
  Boulder, Colorado 80301
  Frederick A. Praeger, Publisher

Library of Congress Catalog Card Number: 80-71079
ISBN: 0-86531-080-7

First published in 1981 in Great Britain by
  André Deutsch Limited
  105 Great Russell Street
  London WC1

Printed and bound in the United States of America

For Richard and Jeannie under whose roof it began and Sherrida who made sure it was finished on time

Contents

List of Plates

(between pages 100 and 101, and 130 and 131)

Photograph number 3 was taken by G.F.R. Sherriff and the remainder of the photographs were taken by J. C. Griffiths.

List of Maps

Introduction

'*Bronyenosni!*' The word seemed incongruous in what should have been a conversation about the design of a commercial vehicle maintenance depot. What could 'armour plate' have to do with those ramshackle pop art extravaganzas that passed for trade trucks and buses in Afghanistan? And why would a road need to withstand a dead axle weight of fifty tons? Overloading was another art at which the Afghans excelled but not to that extent. I edged a little closer to the group of lugubrious looking Russians on whose conversation I was eavesdropping. They saw but ignored me, assuming, I imagined, that I could not understand what they were saying, and continued to grumble about being sent to this one-horse town. I could resist the temptation no longer.

'Good day comrades. And what brings you to Herat?'

Confusion; embarrassment; anger. Would I be supposed to know about the vehicle maintenance project?

'We're . . . er . . . ah . . . − on holiday.'

'I'm sorry you are having such a miserable time,' I commiserated, 'but I just love your holiday clothes.' I took in their identical dungarees, pointed hats and little attache cases with a patronizing sweep.

'I must just get a snap as a souvenir.'

As I raised my camera the leader of the group jumped to his feet and charged towards me waving his fist and shouting '*Niet!*' An hour later I was being questioned by two Russians and an apologetic Afghan policeman who was only too ready to be appeased by my offer to expose the film in my camera – a blank roll substituted long since while the police were being fetched.

That was in 1957. The Russians were among the pioneers of the Soviet aid programme arranged by the autocratic Afghan Premier, Daoud. The project on which they were engaged was indeed one of three vehicle maintenance depots tied in with the road building programme. But I had no doubt that if the time ever came both projects could serve a military purpose. Nor was the British military attaché to whom I recounted my adventures and who had been fruitlessly filing similar reports for some time, in any doubt or the editor of *Illustrated,* who printed my picture and story. But most people treated the incident as no more than a typical traveller's tale.

In 1980 those imaginary tanks of 1957 were standing squat and all too real at every crossroads in Kabul and along every highway in Afghanistan, to reinforce the authority of the fourth dictator to rule that country within the space of the previous two years. As to just how bloody those dictatorships were, let contemporary reports speak for themselves.

'First some thirty members of President Daoud's family were shot before his eyes, also senior members of his government, then Daoud himself was shot.' Diplomatic report. 26 April 1978.

'President Hafizullah Amin's wife, nephew, and seven children, and some twenty or thirty of his aides were shot down when he was killed.' 27 December 1979. *Daily Telegraph* 21 February 1980.

'Since April 1978 there have been more than two hundred and fifty conspiracies and armed attacks against the régime.' President Amin, October 1979.

'Tens of thousands of Afghans were jailed or collectively liquidated by the bloodthirsty hangman Hafizullah Amin.' President Karmal.

'Fifty or sixty Russian men and women were killed and some of them flayed alive.' March 1979.

'This person calls himself a mullah but he destroyed Islam and worked against Muslims.' That rebel verdict condemned the mullah to be burned to death in his own house in Karabagh near Kabul in the Summer of 1979.

'Rebels stoned the Soviet Embassy in Kabul and killed six members of the staff.' 1 October 1979.

'Two hundred men were bound in their own pugris, soaked in petrol and burned to death.' Summer 1979.

'Between April 1978 and September 1979 more than twelve thousand prisoners were held without trial and many of them were tortured.' Amnesty International.

'While the soldiers started pulling down and burning the houses, thirteen children were rounded up and stood in a line in front of their parents. Some of the soldiers then poked out the children's eyes with steel rods. The mutilated children were then slowly strangled to death. Next it was the parents' turn and one by one they were shot, as was everybody in the village. The bodies along with everything else, were burned. The surrounding fields were bulldozed, all trees and shrubs uprooted and the entire site reduced to an ash-strewn scar.' *The Times.* 21 January 1980.

Hearsay and eyewitness, exaggeration and cold fact, it is hard to disentangle the hard truth from amongst the bloody pieces, but that Afghanistan has undergone a reign of terror with atrocities perpetrated on both sides is not in doubt.

1 FULCRUM OF EMPIRES

The events described in the Introduction may shock the western reader accustomed to more peaceful changes of government, but to the inhabitant of Afghanistan they will have seemed no more than a commonplace pattern engrained in his history. The peaks and passes of the Hindu Kush have been the fulcrum by which ambitious powers have tried to lever an empire into their grasp for over two thousand years, long before there was such a country as Afghanistan.

Afghans* are first referred to as a people in the tenth century AD, but as the tribal inhabitants of certain parts of the country now known as Afghanistan, rather than as 'nationals' of the whole country. In the eighteenth and nineteenth centuries, Afghans themselves would have talked of their own regions by tribal names, and any references to the larger area would probably have been to 'Pushtun'. It was only through Persian and English writers that the term 'Afghanistan', and indeed of 'Afghans', first came into general usage, due to the fact that the ruling house was Afghan. Throughout this book, the people of Afghan race are denoted by the Indian

---

*G. Michanovsky suggests that the name derives from the Sanskrit 'Avagana' which in turn goes back to the Sumerian (c 3000 BC) word for the mountainous region of Badakshan, 'Ab-bar-Gan' or 'High Country'.

word 'Pathans'. To call them 'Pushtuns' would imply that they all speak Pushtu, which is not the case. The term 'Afghans' is here made to refer to all citizens of modern Afghanistan, not solely to that racial group to which the term strictly applies. It must be borne in mind that in earlier times no members of the other racial groups would have dreamed of calling themselves Afghans.

The country of the Afghans is one of sharp contrasts in climate, terrain and people. It abounds in deserts of every kind, in the midst of which the traveller comes with eye-catching suddenness on green and fertile valleys or a confetti of purple flowers scattered across seemingly arid soil. In summer he may encounter a heat that seems to make the very flesh singe, while in winter a scimitar wind guards the snow-blocked passes of the mountains that cover so much of the country.

The people vary greatly in stature, colour, race and feature, the ethnic sediment deposited in the tidal wake of at least two thousand years of invasions, sweeping by along the breakwater of the Hindu Kush mountains and towards India. The Hindu Kush cuts Afghanistan virtually in half, running from the thin strip of inaccessible mountains in the north-east that barely separates Russia, China and Pakistan, almost to the empty desert sands of the western border with Iran. South and south-east lie Kandahar, Ghazni and Kabul; to the north Faizabad and Mazar-i-Sharif, and to the west Herat. Northward of these towns, the river Oxus forms much of the border with Russia. In the south of the country, the people are mainly Pathans; in the north, Tajiks, Turkmen, Kirghiz and Uzbegs; and in the central mountains, Hazaras.

Every landward invasion of the subcontinent − save for that of the Arabs, in the eighth century of our era, through the then much more fertile Makran − has pivoted on the south-western end of the Hindu Kush or has

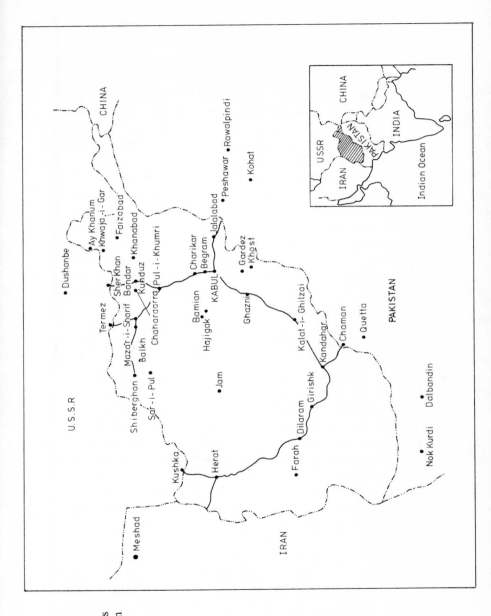

Map 1: Places referred to in the text

filtered, in season, through its high passes. This has given to Herat, Kandahar and Kabul a continental strategic significance. The pattern of invasion and empire has been markedly repetitive. The impulse of the first irresistible thrust south or east; a pivot on the southwestern flank of the Hindu Kush; a brief pause to conquer and consolidate some such vantage point as Ghazni or Kabul; a sweep down into India and a battle in the first open country beyond the Indus, to establish a seat in northern India itself; and then the gradual softening of the conquerors in the enervating climate until they can no longer resist new incursors pressing behind them or are overthrown for a brief interregnum by a locally nurtured dynasty – such, for two millennia, has been the oft-repeated experience of those over whom the endless armies swept.

Sir Olaf Caroe in his history of the Pathans, lists no less than twenty-five dynasties ruling over all or part of what is now Afghanistan, from the Achaemenian dominion of Cyrus and Darius the Great in the sixth century BC to the last of the ruling house of the Barakzai, Prince Daoud, overthrown by the Russian-backed coup of 1978. In the first two millenia of this period, Persian influence was not merely dominant but well-nigh exclusive, for most even of those invaders who were not themselves Persian had undergone the transmutation of contact with Persian culture through either submission or conquest. This Persian influence still pervades Afghan life today, and is perhaps as important as the later influence of Islam.

Of all the conquests of the land of the Afghans, none can match – in military genius, at least – that of Alexander the Great who, in the four years between the battle of Gaugamela in 331 BC and the onset of his India campaign from its base at Alexandria Arachosia (Charikar), conquered the peoples of Khurasan, Transoxiana, and what we now call Afghanistan. He left behind him Greek-garrisoned cities, many bearing his name, which he hoped would be centres of civilized and ordered dominion. Alexander's hopes were not to be fulfilled. He conquered but could not subdue these Central Asian peoples, and no sooner had he died than his lieutenants, the new Hellenistic rulers of the old Persian satrapies, fell out among themselves. None of them was strong enough to achieve an overall control, although Hellenistic kingdoms — such as that of the Seleucids and Graeco-Bactrians — were to survive in small parts of the area for a few more decades.

The significance of Alexander's invasion lies not so much in its military accomplishments, or even in the social influence which, superficially at least, it appears to have had, as in its reversal, for the first time, of the common flow of conquest from the East to the West. Although the sweeping invasions of the hordes of Central Asia were still to come, from now on the peoples of the Mediterranean and the mainland of Europe could turn their eyes eastward, not just to watch for the dust clouds of invasion, but to dream of plunder, profit and glory for themselves.

The Macedonians were ousted by the only empire in this first millennium of our Afghan story to owe nothing to the Persians: the Maurya empire of Chandragupta in India. Under his grandson Asoka, Maurya rule in the second century BC spread the influence of Buddhism throughout this part of Asia. Little evidence, however, of that faith remains in Afghanistan today, save for the great rock-carvings of Bamian, which even the ravages of Genghis Khan could not destroy.

Two other dynasties are worth noting, prior to the coming of Islam. The Graeco-Bactrian empire of Demetrius and Menander centred on Taxila (185–97 BC), though enduring for less than a hundred years, nurtured one of the great artistic flowerings of the ancient world, the sculptures of Gandhara. Although it now appears that many of the accomplishments of Gandharan art were achieved under the following Kushan dynasty, the impetus for this beautiful fusion of Greek and Buddhist art stems from the earlier empire. In the fifth century AD, Bactria was overrun by the White Huns: men of Turkic origin, tall and white-skinned. Checked momentarily by the Sassanid empire in Persia, by the end of the century the White Huns had not only made that empire tributary to their own, but had also mastered northern India, where their rule endured well into the sixth century of our era.

The breakdown of law and order which followed the invasion of the White Huns, perhaps initiated that self-reliant parochialism which is at the root of the fierce tribal and micro-geographical independence and mutual hostility which characterizes the structure of Afghan society in recent centuries. Even the unifying influence of Islam has not been able to break down this attitude.

Contrary to what some Afghan historians would have us believe, Afghanistan was not immediately converted to Islam as soon as the Prophet breathed the word. In fact, the first Muslim régime to control a considerable part of the country (and even then it was fully effective only south of the Hindu Kush) was the Ghaznavid kingdom. The town and province of Ghazni formed a part of the Persian Samanid empire and was governed for them by a series of Turkish mamluks. Sabuktagin, who served the last of these, overthrew his master in 977 and founded the dynasty which he named after the town. Under his son Mahmud it did, indeed, achieve considerable military and cultural renown, but like so many others it was shortlived. It was in Mahmud's reign, however, that Islam was forcibly made the religion of Afghanistan. Ghazni was sacked in 1150 by the otherwise undistinguished (if vainglorious) Tajik, Alauddin Jahansoz — the World Burner, as he liked to be called. With classic cruelty he compelled his captives to each carry a heavy pack of the soil of Ghazni to his capital, Firoz-Koh in the mountains of Ghor. There he butchered his captives, mixed their blood with the soil of their native town, and built victory towers from the mortar thereof. It is hard to believe that such a barbarous tradition should lie behind the seemingly mild and peaceful Tajiks who now farm the countryside north of Kabul, but that they still have the capacity for ferocious deeds is demonstrated by the seizure of the Afghan throne by a Tajik as recently as 1929, and their present fierce resistance, in some areas, to the Russian invaders. For a brief period then, rule over the Ghaznavid empire was borne by the forbears of the present Afghan Tajiks until they were brushed aside by the Mongol hordes of Genghis Khan, who again destroyed Ghazni some seventy years later. Today the town itself, save for the remaining Ghaznavid minarets, is only an unimpressive collection of rather dilapidated buildings.

Before reaching Ghazni in 1221–22, Genghis Khan had already done more razing and ravaging than any man in history before him. Yet it was almost by accident that he came to establish his dreadful rule over so much of this part of Asia. His own home region firmly under his control, he was quite willing to live decently with his neighbour to the West, to whom he sent the following note:

I am the sovereign of the sunrise, and thou the sovereign of the sunset. Let there be between us a firm treaty of friendship, amity and peace, and let traders and caravans on both sides come and go, and let the precious products and ordinary commodities which may be in my territory be conveyed by them into thine, and those in thine to mine.[1]

To give substance to his message he sent a treasure caravan of five hundred camels laden with gold, silver, silk, furs, sable and other 'elegant and ingenious' rarities.

Unfortunately, for the future of Central Asia, a greedy officer in command of the border seized Genghis Khan's treasure and butchered all but one member of Genghis Khan's caravan. When, to add insult to injury, Genghis' messengers demanding recompense were returned with singed beards, he unleashed the devastation with which his name has come to be associated. As Juvaini wrote only thirty years later, 'with one stroke a world which billowed with fertility was laid desolate, and the regions thereof became a desert. . . .'[2] Fraser-Tytler in his history of Afghanistan, did not much exaggerate when he said that 'the Mongol invasions of Central Asia and Europe were, until the rise of the Nazis under Hitler, the greatest catastrophe which has befallen mankind.'[3] In 1220, Genghis Khan crossed the Oxus and sacked the city of Herat, which lies on an open road fifty miles from the present Russian border. He then advanced on the ancient centre of arts and learning in Balkh, so completely devastating this area that the Moroccan traveller Ibn Batuta in 1333, more than a century later, found only rubble and desolation where there had once been great cities. Ghazni itself fell to the lot of Genghis Khan's son Chagatai but he never visited or took interest in this outpost of his domain which, as a centre of arts and learning, had been irrevocably destroyed. But, with ironic justice, the Mongols were to leave even less trace of their achievements, if that is the right word, than did the kingdoms they laid waste. The only enduring, positive witnesses to their invasions are the colonies of Mongol Hazaras in west-central Afghanistan: a land of narrow valleys, rugged blocks of mountains and swift turbulent rivers, in keeping with the nature of the inhabitants who are aggressive and constantly at odds with the other peoples of the country.

Yet Afghanistan, reduced to an even more complete state of anarchy than usual, had not yet done with the Mongols, or at least with a Turco-Iranian branch of them. In 1379 Tamerlane crossed the Oxus by a bridge of boats at Termez, one of the few practicable points and today the main port for Russia's invading army; nineteen years later, his cavalry crossed the Khawak Pass en route for India. In Afghanistan itself, he even mounted a campaign against the tribesmen in the wild and mountainous country north-east of Kabul. Termed 'Kafirs' by the Muslim faithful, their land, 'Kafiristan' — the Land of the Unbelievers — is now, since they embraced Islam at sword point in 1895, more felicitously known as Nuristan — the Land of Light. It was on this campaign that Tamerlane and his men tobogganed recklessly down a mountainside on their shields to attack the enemy!

Tamerlane's was a very different empire from that of his Mongol predecessors, based as it was on Samarkand — so richly and beautifully embellished by the buildings and works of art commissioned by the lame conqueror. Other cities, like Herat, became flourishing centres of the arts under his immediate successors. It was the determination to regain Samarkand and restore its glories that obsessed Babur — descended from both Tamerlane and Genghis Khan — before he realized that the ambition was a hopeless one, and instead turned his thoughts towards India. Although for many years after the loss of his kingdom in Ferghana, Babur still pursued his youthful dreams, in the end the relentless logic of the south-ward advance of the Uzbegs under Shaibani Khan forced him to seek a kingdom in Kabul and the lands beyond the Indus. Shaibani Khan bequeathed to Afghanistan the Uzbeg people still living in the northern part of the country, while Babur went on to found one of the world's most magnificent empires, that of the Mogul dynasty in India.

For once, Kabul fell into a new ruler's hands without a struggle, in October 1504*. 'So, towards the end of [this] month', wrote Babur in his memoirs, 'by the blessing of Almighty God I obtained and subjected Kabul and Ghazni with their provinces without effort or battle.'⁴ (If Babur made history on the grand scale, he also wrote it with the delightful personal touch we find in the *Babur-nama*.) He clearly recognized the strategic advantages of Kabul. Successful raids on India might be made from any centre in southern Afghanistan, but Kabul must be securely held for the permanent conquest of northern India. ('Indian' empires of the various Asiatic conquerors never had sufficient impetus to embrace the whole of southern India.) Yet for Babur the attractions of Kabul − which, as one legend has it, was founded by and named after Cain − were far more than that of mere strategic advantage. 'From Kabul', wrote Babur, 'you can go in a single day to a place where the snow never falls, and in two hours you can also reach a place where the snow never melts, except at times in a particularly hot summer.'⁵ The qualification shows the typical realism of the man who saw that Kabul was 'a land to be governed by the sword, not the pen.'

That twenty-one years elapsed between Babur's cap-

---

*The fact that Babur's uncle, Ulugh Beg, had held the city for thirty-two years, until 1501, may account in part for the ease of its capture.

ture of Kabul and his conquest of India in December 1525, with an army of less than twelve thousand men, was due to the difficulty of consolidating his base from Kandahar to Kabul. This proved a laborious task in the face of the hostility of the hill tribes: those men whom Ibn Batuta had described as 'a tribe of Persians called Afghans. They hold mountains and defiles, possess considerable strength, and are mostly highwaymen.'6 Indeed, it may be that the decision to turn his attention to building up an empire in India was influenced by his inability completely to subdue the Pathan tribesmen. These, he realized, he might contain but never control. The turbulent and independent spirit of these tribal peoples is one of the great constants of Afghanistan's history. They have changed little, despite the many invasions, since the time of Alexander.

However this may be, Babur finally penetrated into north India, and at much-embattled Panipat, site of so many contests for the mastery of India, gained the brilliant and decisive victory which was to give him the throne of Delhi. By placing the centre of his empire in that city, he made Afghanistan once more the northern outpost of an Indian empire, as in the days of the Maurya dynasty, and with the inevitable debilitating consequences. The Mogul succession in India was dramatically, if only temporarily, interrupted by Sher Shah – probably the most outstanding of the many Afghans to have carved out kingdoms away from their native land. (Sher Shah himself reigned in Delhi for only six years – from 1539 to 1545 – his successors reigned for a further ten years.) Although the reign of Babur's son Humayun was shaken for only a few years, he and his greater descendants were never able to establish complete control over Afghanistan, much of which eventually came once more under the influence of Persia.

It was after a further two hundred years of petty tribal intrigue and conflict that this same Persian influence became indirectly responsible for the creation of modern Afghanistan.

On a clear June night in 1747, the army of Nadir Shah of Persia, whose conquests had ranged from Turkey to India, lay encamped not far from Meshed in northern Persia. Its royal commander had decided to punish a rebellious Kurdish tribe which had attacked his stud farm at Radkan. For this rebellion – and it was but one of many at the time – Nadir Shah had only his own increasing mental derangement to blame, for it was leading him into cruelties horrifying even by the standards of a cruel age. A French priest who accompanied the Shah records that 'wherever he had halted he had many people tortured and put to death, and had towers of their heads erected.'

Ahmad Khan, an Afghan noble in his early twenties, sat outside his tent in the Shah's encampment, reflecting on the circumstances that had brought him, the son of one of Nadir's defeated opponents, into the Persian monarch's personal staff at the age of sixteen to become, now, the commander of that Afghan contingent, four thousand strong, which had served in the van of so many of the Shah's campaigns.

An excited messenger from Nadir broke into his meditations. Ahmad was to arm his Afghans, arrest all the officers of the Shah's personal bodyguard in the morning, and take over the guard duties himself. His master – always discovering plots, some real, some imagined – had that day learned of a conspiracy against him. He had tried to flee the camp but the guards had dissuaded him with protestations of loyalty. Yet it was the commander of the guard who was the chief instigator of the plot, and the Shah was taking no chances. The conspirators were to be put in irons.

Unfortunately for the Shah, his instructions to Ahmad were overheard by an agent of the conspirators; they realized that their only hope lay in immediate action in anticipation of the counterplot. Many of them backed out in the crisis, but a handful made their way into Nadir's tent past the acquiescent guard. One conspirator slashed off the hand that the Shah raised to protect himself, another then struck off his head. The murder — perhaps tyrannicide would be a fairer word — had to be kept secret from the Afghan and Uzbeg troops so that these could be taken unawares in the morning. But Ahmad Khan was to benefit from having a friend in the right place. One of Nadir Shah's widows was able to get a message to him about the attack. Such a thing seemed incredible; even so, Ahmad stood his men to arms all night and at first light ordered them to the Shah's tent to establish the accuracy of the report. At the women's quarters further advance was barred by the Turkmen guards who were plundering the camp indiscriminately, but the Afghans fought their way through to learn for themselves that they had been told the truth.

By now, the gallimaufry of disparate tribal contingents was seizing the chance to settle old scores. A dozen minor battles flared throughout the camp. In the confusion of Nadir Shah's instantly disintegrating empire, Ahmad and his followers hacked their way out of the camp and began their march home — taking the fabulous Koh-i-Noor diamond with them. By the time they neared their destination, Kandahar, the members of the Afghan force, drawn from a variety of tribes, had reached the conclusion that they now owed no allegiance to a Persian suzerain and should claim independence under their own elected chief. But who was this chief to be?

The story has it that for eight long sessions they debated the matter, during all of which time Ahmad Khan said not a word. Then, in the ninth session, as the argument slackened through sheer weariness, the darvesh Sabir Shah jumped to his feet to advance Ahmad Khan's claims. 'Why all this verbosity? God has created Ahmad Khan a much greater man than any of you. His is the most noble of all the Afghan families. Maintain, therefore, God's work, for His wrath will weight heavily on you if you destroy it.' While this account may seem an unlikely tale, clearly Ahmad Khan — or Ahmad Shah Durr-i-Durran (Pearl of Pearls) as he now became — had already made a great impression on his fellow Afghans by his ability and personality. This impression he was quickly to enhance by his subsequent actions.

No sooner had Ahmad entered Kandahar than he managed to seize a treasure caravan of tribute bound for Nadir Shah. This he generously and shrewdly distributed among the Afghan chiefs. It was also psychologically astute of him to give the new name of Durrani to his own tribe, the Abdali, thus identifying them with himself and not with past feuds, quarrels and jealousies. In the course of the next twenty-six years, his military and political genius was to create an Afghanistan that was, for the first time, a distinct political entity in Central Asia, and a clearly recognizable progenitor of present-day Afghanistan.

Ahmad Shah's principal objective was to unite the various Afghan peoples. He realized that this unity could only be achieved by a loosely-knit system — a sort of feudal federalism — in which the independent prerogatives of the tribal chiefs would remain unimpugned by the central power provided they gave it military support. At the same time, it was at least partly to guard against possible rivals that he appointed prominent members of his family to important posts, which became virtually hereditary: a practice not unknown in modern Afghanistan. He went a step further, and constituted a Majlis (or council) of nine chiefs which played a genuinely in-fluential part in policy-making. Though he could, and did, deal severely with the more blatant and persistent offenders against his régime, he also gained a reputation for remarkable clemency in an age not renowned for that virtue in Asia.

The second major instrument of Ahmad Shah's policy of unification was the age-old device of foreign con-quest. This has been well described by Mountstuart Elphinstone in his perceptive *Account of the Kingdom of Caubul.*

> For the consolidation of his power at home he relied in great measure on the effects of his foreign wars. If these were successful, his victories would raise his reptuation, and his conquests would supply him with the means of maintaining an army, and of attaching the Afghan chiefs by favour and rewards; the hopes of plunder would induce many tribes to join him, whom he could not easily have compelled to submit; by carrying the great men with his army he would be able to prevent their increasing, or even preserving, their influence in their tribes; and the habits of military obedience would prepare them for a cheerful sub-mission to his government at home; the troops also, having the King constantly before their eyes, and witnessing the submission of their hereditary chiefs, would learn to regard him as the head of the nation; and he might hope, as the event proved, that his popular manners, and the courage, activity, vigilance and other military virtues which he possessed, would impress all ranks with respect, and strongly attach his soldiers to his person.[7]

Ahmad Shah's first step after taking power in Kan-dahar in 1747 was to subdue Kabul, and Ghazni en route. Before the end of the year, less than six months after coming to power, he had set out on the first of those eight invasions of India that were to fulfil so successfully the policy described by Elphinstone.

However, fortunately for the future of his own country, he had no ambition or desire, as had so many previous invaders of the subcontinent, to transfer his seat of government to Delhi and to rule India. Ahmad Shah's interest was in conquest, not empire, and after his campaigns he always returned to Kabul. It is doubtful whether he would have maintained his kingdom from a capital in Delhi. Afghanistan at this time was fortunately relieved of external pressures by the disintegration earlier in the century of the Mogul and the Persian Safavid empires, and the Sikhs had not yet become established. Although Ahmad Shah generally defeated his Indian opponents (principally Sikhs and Marathas) in battle, they flowed in again like puddle water behind his wagon wheels as soon as he marched on. He could not maintain permanent lines of communication across territory still in the hands of such formidable opponents. He returned to his own country after each invasion to consolidate his domestic position and to extend the other frontiers of his empire. In the early years of his reign he added to his dominions northwards Bamian and Badakshan, and across the Oxus, Khurasan.

When Ahmad Shah died at the age of fifty, from a particularly unpleasant combination of diabetes and an ulcerating nose wound, the old-style internecine struggle for power immediately broke out again among his sons, and gradually his empire crumbled.

In 1818, after a series of particularly barbaric plots and counterplots in which blinding of opponents was a routine feature, the successors of Ahmad Shah were ousted by the Muhammadzai Barakzai clan. The ancestor of this clan, a group within the Durrani tribe, had stood down in the leadership contest from which

Ahmad Shah emerged as the chosen chief of the Afghans. It was during the disputes over the succession in the first quarter of the last century that the Punjab and Peshawar were finally lost to the Afghan kingdom. The Barakzai, the second branch of whom provided the last monarch, had very strong emotional ties with Peshawar, the winter capital of its ancestors until wrested from them by Sikh arms. This close dynastic association with a 'lost province' was possibly in the minds of those early Victorians like Alexander Burnes, who believed that stability in this part of the world depended on the restoration of Peshawar to the Durrani kingdom. It was a contributory factor in the persistent irredentism in subsequent Afghan monarchs.

The kingdom which Ahmad Shah had carved out for himself did have certain elements of cohesion. Save for its tenuously held regions in Khurasan and east of the Khyber, in the Punjab and southwards in Baluchistan and Sind, Ahmad Shah's realm covered, broadly speaking, the area of present-day Afghanistan. That it required external compression, to be applied by the advancing empires of Britain and Russia, to make these elements of cohesion ultimately effective, is the next major part of Afghanistan's history.

2 THE GREAT GAME

With the founding of the Mogul empire by Babur, the centuries of pre-eminence of the horse-bowmen of Central Asia came to an end. Not until the Chinese incursion of 1962 would India again be invaded from Central Asia. But, if the great subcontinent was now secure from attack from the north, at the courts of the Great Mogul emperors there appeared – outwardly diffident and deferential, at heart observant, curious and ambitious – the outriders of a far more powerful invasion from a different direction and of a different kind.

By the mid-eighteenth century, at the time when the Afghans were forming their first independent kingdom under Ahmad Shah, the British were establishing themselves firmly, under the aegis of the East India Company, in substantial parts of India. As mercantile interests developed into political involvement, so the latter engendered a British military presence, first in conflict with the rival power of France and its Indian allies and then, after the defeat of France, with the native principalities themselves. Thus the British found themselves constantly obliged to extend the areas under their military control in order to maintain the stability necessary for prosperous trade. The British advance towards the frontiers of Afghanistan, both by means of diplomacy and war, culminated in the first and second Sikh wars (1845 and 1849). These, by breaking the power of Ranjit Singh's successors, brought British rule right up to the borders of Afghanistan.

Nor was Britain alone in extending its power towards Afghanistan, although Russia's expansion to its southeast did not get under way until almost a generation after the consolidation of the British presence in northern India. During the first half of the nineteenth century, the Russians were engaged in taking over the Kirghiz steppes, and were still a long way from their present frontiers with Afghanistan. Their ventures in this part of the world had to be conducted at second hand. In 1838, they persuaded the Persians to lay siege to the strategically situated city of Herat. The implications of this seemed clear. A British diplomat with the Persian army, who was trying to persuade the Shah to abandon the project, observed in a report: 'The fall of Herat would destroy our position in Afghanistan and place nearly all that country under the influence or authority of Russia and Persia.'¹ However, the defence of Herat, courageously conducted under the leadership of a young British lieutenant* who had just arrived in the city, was stubborn and the city held out until Britain's threat of war forced the Shah to break off the operation and withdraw his army, thus temporarily thwarting Russian ambitions in the area.

Russia's aims at the time were mainly commercial, if a dispatch dated 20 October 1838, from Count Nesselrode, the Russian Foreign Minister, to his Ambassador in London is to be believed. It refers to the

. . . indefatigable activity displayed by English travellers in spreading disquiet among the people of Central Asia, and

---

*Eldred Pottinger, whose exciting subsequent career, before dying young of a fever, included survival of the retreat from Kabul in 1842 and—with one other man only—of the massacre at Charikar which immediately preceded it.

in carrying agitation even into the heart of the countries bordering on our frontiers; while on our part we ask nothing but to be admitted to [share] in fair competition the commercial advantages of Asia. English industry, exclusive and jealous, would deprive us entirely of the benefits which it [claims] to reap alone; and would cause, if it could, the produce of our manufacturers to disappear from all the markets of Central Asia.[2]

Dust Mohammed was the able ruler who had emerged from the anarchy of the first quarter of the nineteenth century to govern Afghanistan at this formative time. He ousted the Saddozai descendants of Ahmad Shah to become the first of the Barakzai clan to hold the throne. Anxious though he was to secure British friendship, he never met with the response he deserved from the Raj. Lord Auckland, the Governor-General of India during this period, imperfectly appreciated the significance of events in Afghanistan or the importance of at least a prophylactic friendship with the Dust — as he was known to the British — in countering Russian ambitions.

Auckland embarked on an intrigue with the Sikh leader, Ranjit Singh, to place a puppet ruler, Shah Shuja, on the Afghan throne. He thus launched Britain on the first of the three Afghan wars that were to prove so disastrous for its relations with Afghanistan.

The pattern of events is worth examining in some detail, because its parallels with present Russian policy are not just academic exercises for the historian, but a source of inspiration for the present Afghan freedom fighters. Their confidence that the Russians cannot impose a government on their country is derived in part from the fact that the great world power of the nineteenth and earlier twentieth century failed three times in such an attempt.

Shah Shuja briefly occupied the throne in Kabul in the

opening decade of the century before fleeing to comfortable exile in India, whence he made one or two half-hearted attempts to regain his kingdom. It was from this retirement that the British and their temporary allies, the Sikhs, dug him out when Russian threats, through the instrument of Persia, appeared to imperil the security of the region. Dust Mohammed himself desired nothing so much as to remain independent of all the great powers. However, for appearance sake, the British accused him of irredentism and 'ambition injurious to the security and peace of the frontiers of India'. Shah Shuja, eager to regain a throne by any means, readily forswore all such 'ambition' and indeed agreed to pay tribute to the Sikhs as well. The British, like the Russians now, claimed that they were not invading Afghanistan but supporting Shuja's troops 'against foreign interference and factious opposition'. Shah Shuja was crowned with great pomp at Kandahar in April 1839, but as Captain Havelock wrote at the time '. . . unless I have been deceived all the national enthusiasm of the scene was entirely confined to his Majesty's immediate retainers. The people of Kandahar viewed the whole affair with the most mortifying indifference.'[3] The ceremony at Kabul later in the year had much the same hollow ring. Clearly the British would have, after all, to maintain their military presence if their protégé was to remain in power. They built cantonments in Kabul and Kandahar and supported garrisons at Girishk, Kalat-i-Ghilzai, Jalalabad, Ghazni, and Charikar, but beyond these towns Shuja's writ did not run. The countryside was in open rebellion and Dust Mohammed's victory at Charikar — though for some inexplicable reason he surrendered to the British after it — was herald of a 'signal catastrophe' yet to come. After uprisings in Kabul and the provinces and the murder first of Sir Alexander Burnes, then of the obtuse Sir William Macnaghten, the British forces beat a precipitate, ill-managed, and sometimes shameful retreat in the bitter January weather of 1842. They lost an entire army, all but the handful of men and women held by local chiefs, and the subsequently celebrated Dr Brydon, in one of the worst disasters in British military history – one which they needs must avenge.

After their victory the tribes rapidly resumed their old rivalries which often erupted into open fighting. The British were not slow to take ruthless advantage of these divisions. By the autumn of 1842, Kabul was retaken and Dust Mohammed had been quietly allowed to resume his throne. British retribution ranged from the senseless and rather petty burning of the old bazaar in Kabul to Major General Knott's butchering of 'every man, woman and child within the village of Killah-Chuk', near Ghazni, in revenge for the wiping out of a detachment of his men. It is not perhaps surprising that the heritage of hatred and distrust the British created for themselves in the nineteenth century was to last, to some extent, even to the present day.

Today, with one significant difference, the pattern is much the same – only the names have changed. The Russians, however, are unlikely to suffer a major military defeat at the hands of the Afghan freedom fighters, such is the disparity in weapons and resources, and even less likely to retreat until they have what they want.

The first Afghan war was followed by seventy years of vacillation in British policy for, even in the high noon of expansionism in the latter half of the nineteenth century, there were strong differences of opinion regarding Afghanistan. Things looked very different from the respective vantage points of London and Delhi, while the changes of political power in England between half-hearted Imperialists and ill-informed Liberals made the .

pursuit of a consistent policy almost impossible.

Those – like Lord Roberts and the Duke of Cambridge – who favoured an active British presence in Afghanistan, supported what came to be known as the 'forward policy', which accepted the logic of imperial necessity. India could not be defended along its existing frontiers, hence it was essential – so the argument ran – to push those frontiers forward to the natural barriers of the Hindu Kush. Only thus could authority and jurisdiction over the wild frontier tribes be established, and Afghans be convinced of the advisability of throwing in their lot with the British, and the Indian empire be secured. Had the forward policy been put fully into operation in an avowedly imperialist mood, it is at least arguable that the stability of the area would today be greater than it is. But Liberal opinion rejected this policy outright, chiefly because of its belief that aggressive wars were morally indefensible; and also, perhaps, in reaction to the secondary argument of the 'forward school', that control of the tribal areas would provide the British army with a new recruiting source of good fighting men, loyal cannon-fodder for the Raj.

When in power, the Liberals tried to reverse decisions and dispositions made in the name of the forward policy, some of them going so far as to suggest that, if a natural frontier were required for India, Britain would do well to withdraw to the Indus.* They did not perhaps fully appreciate the bloody consequences of such a

---

*In view of the criticism of this Liberal advocacy of the southerly 'realistic' frontier on the Indus, it is only fair to note that this policy was not simply a notion dreamed up in remote London by what Imperialists call the 'Perish India' school of radicals. First suggested by Sir James Outram, the celebrated Political Agent, in 1854, the Indus frontier line was also advocated by other men on the spot, including Sir John (later Lord) Lawrence, Governor-General, 1863–68.

withdrawal. The hill tribesmen, left to their own devices, would take their traditional road of plunder and depredation, and this in all probability would provoke the traditional response of brutal reprisals and punitive expeditions. Even so, it was Liberal opinion which, by promoting the concept of a buffer state, was to some extent responsible for the creation of modern Afghanistan – although one need not go so far as Sir Thomas Holdich who at the turn of the century wrote:

> We have contributed much to give a national unity to that nebulous community which we call Afghanistan (but which Afghans never call by that name) by drawing a boundary all round it and elevating it into the position of a buffer state between ourselves and Russia. What is there about Afghanistan to guarantee its continued existence as a buffer state between England and Russia? No other country in the world is interested in its prolonged existence except these two. Afghanistan, as a national entity, can only exist by favour of military support of one or the other of them. We need hardly enquire on which side the burden will always lie.[4]

There is a nice irony in this last remark. During the second half of the nineteenth century, the Russians moved inexorably southward into central Asia under the leadership of such brilliant generals and administrators as Kaufman and Skobelev. The logic and justification of this advance was set out in a memorandum of the Russian Chancellor, Prince Gorchakov, in 1864; in a different geographical context, it might have come from the pen of a British minister:

> The position of Russia in Central Asia is that of all civilized states which come into contact with half savage, wandering tribes possessing no fixed social organization.
> It invariably happens in such cases that the interests of

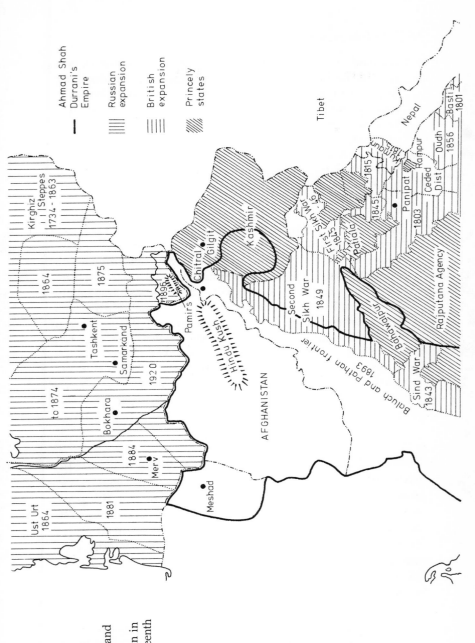

Map 2:
Russian and
British
expansion in
the nineteenth
century

Ahmad Shah
Durrani's
Empire

Russian
expansion

British
expansion

Princely
states

Kirghiz
i I Steppes
1734 – 1863

1864

1875

Tashkent

Samarkand

to 1874

Bokhara

1920

1884

Merv

Meshad

Pamirs

1896

Chitral

Gilgit

Kashmir

Hindu Kush

AFGHANISTAN

Second
Sikh War
1849

Baluch and Pathan frontier
1893

Sind War
1843

Bahawalpur

First Sikh War
1845-46

Punjab

Patiala

1815

Panipat

1803

Ceded
Dist

Rumpur

Oudh
1856

Basti
1801

Rajputana Agency

Tibet

Nepal

Ust Urt
1864

1881

security on the frontier, and of commercial relations, compel the more civilized states to exercise a certain ascendancy over neighbours whose turbulence and nomad instincts render them difficult to live with. First we have incursions and pillage to repress. In order to stop these, we are compelled to reduce the tribes on our frontiers to a more or less complete submission. Once this result is attained they become less troublesome, but in their turn they are exposed to the aggression of more distant tribes. The state is obliged to defend them against these depredations and to chastise those who commit them. Hence the necessity of distant and costly expeditions, repeated at frequent intervals, against an enemy whose whole social organization enables him to elude pursuit. If we content ourselves with chastising the freebooters and then retire, the lesson is soon forgotten. Retreat is ascribed to weakness, for Asiatics respect only visible and palpable force; that arising from the exercise of reason and a regard for the interest of civilization has as yet no hold over them. The task has, therefore, to be performed over again. The United States in America, France in Algeria, Holland in her colonies, England in India — all have been inevitably drawn to a course wherein ambition plays a smaller part than imperious necessity and where the greatest difficulty is knowing where to stop.[5]

Soon Britain was also to return full-bloodedly to the forward policy which had been in abeyance as a consequence of the Indian Mutiny of 1857 and of the prevalence of the Liberal attitudes at home. In 1876, Disraeli appointed Lord Lytton to be Viceroy of India, with a clear brief to reinstate the forward policy. A memorandum of instructions clearly summarized the situation Lytton was sent to change, and he was asked to consider

the probable influence of that situation upon the uncertain character of an oriental chief whose ill-defined dominions

are thus brought within a steadily narrowing circle between the conflicting pressures of two great military empires, one of which expostulates and remains passive,
while the other apologizes and continues to move forward.[6]

As a result of Lytton's close adherence to his instructions, Britain was soon embroiled in a second Afghan
war (1878–79). This was successful militarily, a swiftly
moving campaign leading to the capture of such key
points as Kabul and Kandahar. Indeed, in 1879 or 1880,
the British very likely could have taken over the control
and administration of Afghanistan south of the Hindu
Kush, thereby bringing the forward policy, of which
Lytton was so staunch a supporter, to its logical conclusion. Yet Disraeli's Viceroy got cold feet and looked for a
way out of assuming for Britain *de facto* responsibility
for the area. Although an ardent forwardist, in the first
three months of 1880 Lytton realized that his speculative
plans for breaking up Afghanistan could only involve
the same tragic disasters as those experienced in Lord
Auckland's time, and would also place an intolerable
burden on both Treasury and Army. He perhaps now
recognized, as so many others had before him, the difference between defeating and controlling the Afghan
tribes.

The change in policy was finally clinched when
Gladstone defeated Disraeli in the election of March
1880 and sent the Marquess of Ripon to replace Lytton
as Viceroy. Indeed, British policy towards Afghanistan
had been a major issue in the election, and the Liberal
'regressive' view had been eloquently put by Gladstone
in one of his Midlothian speeches:

Remember, the sanctity of life in the hill villages of
Afghanistan among the winter snows is as inviolable in the
eye of almighty God as can be your own. Remember that

> He who has united you as human beings in the same flesh
> and blood, has bound you by the law of mutual love, is not
> limited by the shores of this island, is not limited by the
> bounds of Christian civilization; that it passes over the
> whole surface of the earth, and embraces the meanest
> along with the greatest in its unmeasured scope.[7]

With the Conservative defeat, it was these impeccable
– if rather generalized – sentiments which became the
motivating force behind British policy in India and
displaced the forward policy. Writing to the new
Viceroy in May 1880, Lord Hartington, Secretary of
State for India in the new Gladstone administration, was
terse and to the point in his estimate of what had been
gained by the second Afghan war:

> Thus it appears that as the result of two successful cam-
> paigns, of the employment of an enormous force, and of the
> expenditure of large sums of money, all that has yet been
> accomplished has been the disintegration of the state which
> it was desired to see strong, friendly and independent, the
> assumption of fresh and unwelcome liabilities in regard to
> one of its provinces, and a condition of anarchy throughout
> the remainder of the country.[8]

It was fortunate for Britain that at this juncture there
came to the Afghan throne one of its greatest occupants:
Abdur Rahman, one of the few men who could have restored the measure of stability to Afghanistan so essential to British policy. By 1881, the policy of the buffer
state was again in operation, applied by a Liberal
government in the hope, rather than the assurance, that
the Afghans would resist the Russians as vigorously as
they had the British. Such conflict as there was between
the great powers was still at second hand, as at Herat
forty years earlier, only now it was a British protégé who

was worsted when the Russians, in 1885, after occupying the oasis of Merv in the previous year, soundly defeated a large Afghan army barring their final advance up to the river Oxus.

On the last day of March of that year, the Russians attacked and seized the Afghan-held Panjdeh oasis at the very time when London and St. Petersburg were negotiating the precise demarcation of the new frontier between Russia and Afghanistan. That this was not intended to be the final Russian goal was made quite clear in the newspaper *Novosti* shortly afterwards. Herat lay within temptingly easy grasp, and *Novosti* urged that Russia must press on to occupy the city and so 'pierce a window' looking south-eastwards, a convenient halting place for a still further advance towards the Indian Ocean in fulfilment of Russia's 'historic destiny'. The tzarist government may well have reckoned that, with the anti-imperialist Liberals in power in Britain, it could steal a march on the negotiations, and gain a useful strategic position, by a coup de force. If so, they were deceived. Gladstone sought for and obtained from Parliament a war credit of £11 million. For several weeks it seemed possible that Britain would go to war with Russia; but eventually the latter climbed down. The diplomats of the two countries returned to their task of defining the boundaries of the Amir of Afghanistan's dominions: a definition which, in fact, gave Panjdeh to the Russians in exchange for various salients of territory on the Amir's side of the Oxus.

Nothing gives a clearer indication of where the real sovereignty of Afghanistan lay at this time than these and later boundary negotiations between Britain and Russia. The Afghans were mere spectators, while the government of the Chinese empire refused to take part in the boundary demarcation discussions in 1895 over the small area of the Wakhan affecting its border. From 1889, the British and Chinese governments had been resisting Russian incursion into the Pamirs, a mountainous region (the 'Roof of the World') where the two new empires in Asia met the oldest surviving empire of the continent at the north-western extension of the Tibetan tableland. The Pamir Convention of 1895 between Britain and Russia settled the Wakhan question to the satisfaction of London and St. Petersburg, and official circles there felt small concern at the absence of an endorsement of the new demarcation by the government of the decaying Chinese empire. It was not until November 1963 that Peking finally recognized its frontier with Afghanistan as determined by the Pamir Convention — thereby surrendering the line of argument, so far as Afghanistan is concerned, that the Chinese People's Republic has adhered to in regard to the Simla Convention of 1914 which defined the Indo-Tibetan frontier but which, never formally ratified by the imperial government of China, has therefore been held invalid by the Chinese ever since. This Tibetan boundary question, product of the Simla Convention, became a *casus belli* in 1962. It is unlikely but not impossible that the Afghan boundary, demarcated by the Pamir Convention, could become a source of conflict between China and Afghanistan.

An equally troublesome boundary was demarcated in 1893, equally arbitrarily, on the eastern and southern borders of Afghanistan. The Durand Line (named after the British administrator responsible for devising it) is a topographically convenient foothill boundary which cuts right across ethnic and tribal divisions. This political severance of the Pathan tribes on either side of it — a severance they have been inclined to ignore at will — not only gave rise to a whole genre of early twentieth-

century schoolboy fiction but has since bitterly embroiled the governments of Pakistan and Afghanistan,
between which countries the Durand Line now runs.

Sir Olaf Caroe has cogently argued (in an appendix to
the present author's *Afghanistan,* Pall Mall, 1967, for example) that the Durand Line is far less arbitrary than it
may appear. The intention of the colonial officials who
drew it up in 1893, was to divide the tribes which looked
naturally south and east to Peshawar, Kohat, and Quetta,
on what is now the Pakistan side of the border, from the
Afghan tribes whose focus was on Kabul, Ghazni and
Kandahar.

The planting of boundary posts on the northern frontier of Afghanistan by the joint Anglo-Russian commission was something more than a topographical exercise;
it indicated the tacit if limited agreement of two mutually suspicious powers to recognize the confines of
their respective spheres of influence. Thus Holdich
could calmly note, having described Herat and Quetta as
the two hinges of the gate to India: '. . . these two doors
are locked, there is nothing in this year of grace 1900
that need cause us any apprehension for the future safety
of the country'.[9]

Although the opportunity for effective exercise of any
forward policy was gone for good by the turn of the century, its advocates were still promoting it. The Hon.
George Curzon, (as he then was) waxed eloquent in *The
Times* shortly before becoming Viceroy of India:

> Russia has, by the Pamir Convention concluded with Great
> Britain, just come into possession of three-fourths of the
> whole territory known as the Pamirs, and of a position
> which brings her down to the main stream of the Oxus.
> Locally, this involves a great extension of her military and
> political prestige. If at the very same moment that she is

thus permitted to advance up to the Hindu Kush on the north, Great Britain voluntarily retires from a position which she has occupied for ten years on the south, but one interpretation will be placed upon this coincidence by the natives of those regions. They do not understand high diplomacy, and they do not read the letters of retired governors and generals in *The Times*. But with one alphabet they are perfectly familiar, and its two symbols are forward and backward. They will say that Russia is the winning and Britain the receding power.[10]

Lord Roberts spoke as earnestly, if less eloquently, in the House of Lords:

The forward policy, in other words the policy of endeavouring to extend our influence over, and establish law and order on, that part of the border where anarchy, murder and robbery up to the present time have reigned supreme, a policy which has been attended with the happiest results in Baluchistan and the Gilgit frontier — is necessitated by the incontrovertible fact that a great military power is now within striking distance of our Indian possessions and in immediate contact with the state, for the integrity of which we have made ourselves responsible. Some forty years ago the policy of non-interference with the tribes, so long as they did not trouble us, may have been wise and prudent, though selfish and not altogether worthy of a great civilizing power.[11]

But the necessities of European politics were changing and no longer sustained the same degree of confrontation on the frontiers of Central Asia. Indeed, Russia and Britain, sharing a common fear of the growing military strength of imperial Germany in Europe and a common uneasiness over its ambitious diplomatic and commercial forays into the Near East, became allies in 1907 in association with France. The two great Asian empires settled down to administer their respective territories round the frontiers of Afghanistan in ways that sometimes were very similar and sometimes exhibited revealing differences.

One common factor, giving each imperial régime an apparently perennial vigour, was the supply line to the home country for recruitment – in Britain's case by sea, in Russia's by the network of railways reaching to the remotest corners of its southern provinces. A revolution in communications had brought about what numerous revolutions in military technology and tactics had failed to achieve. For the first time, there were now empires in this part of Asia whose rulers did not go into an enervated decline within a few generations since they were constantly refreshed by transfusions of blood kept fresh in the climatic and moral refrigerators of northern Europe. Such empires would endure, or pass away only through voluntary relinquishment.

In conception, the imperial ideals of Britain and Russia might seem very similar. An enlightened Russian colonial administrator could write in his memoirs after the Russian annexation of Transcaspia:

> The entry of Russia into Central Asia, followed by the introduction of European methods and civilization, brought a breath of fresh air to a land despoiled and impoverished by centuries of Asian despotic rule. The reader, accustomed to differentiate between what he has been taught to regard as Western civilization and conditions in Russia, may fail to appreciate the magnitude and effect of the changes wrought in the life of Central Asia by tzarist and autocratic Russia. Slavery was brought to an end; the arbitrary legislation of the Khans, Emirs, and their puppets, the Beks, who controlled a large part of their masters' wealth, such as their flocks, was superseded by Russian law, under which all the inhabitants, irrespective of their standing, were

equal. Hitherto enslaved captives from every race in Asia, emancipated overnight, hastened home to spread the news of these wondrous changes, introduced by a humane administration, upheld by one universal writ, and enforced by Russian arms. Henceforth, the verdicts of the *kadis* (judges) in the local courts were based on the wise adaptation of the *Shari'at* (the holy law of Islam) to the Russian conception of justice.[12]

Would a member of the Indian Civil Service have differed much from this in his description of what he believed British rule to be achieving in India?

In Russia, however, the disease of bureaucracy spread even more virulently than it did in British India. Moreover, into Russia's southern empire poured an influx of colonial settlers from the poorer and tougher sections of Russian society, and these were not going to allow any nice regard for native susceptibilities to hamper their determination to make good. Britain, in India at least, was not faced with the same problem, for there the empire-builders were in the main dedicated career-officers who returned to their own country on completing their service. The Russians tended to despise the British, in the first place for not putting their colonies to better commercial use, and secondly for not imposing outright their own laws and customs on the subject peoples. Russianize, not liberalize, was the formula for tzarist imperialism: a formula the Soviets were not reluctant to inherit. (Forty percent of the present population of Soviet Central Asia is of Russian origin.)

By the beginning of the twentieth century, then, a military and diplomatic stalemate had been reached as if by a kind of Newtonian Third Law of politics. Between the two equal and opposite forces lay Afghanistan.

It was probably fortunate for the great powers bickering over Afghanistan that, during the nineteenth and much of the twentieth centuries, the country's potential leaders were preoccupied with throne-hunting.

The age-old pattern of clan, family and personal rivalry for power was aggravated by the attempts of outside powers, the British in particular, to manipulate Afghan rulers to their own ends. The importance of personal magnetism and leadership was, and is, greater in Afghanistan than in most countires. During the nineteenth century, Abdur Rahman (1880–1901) was the only man of sufficient stature to negotiate with the British the kind of independence which until recently the country enjoyed. But with Russia troubling his northern frontiers, even after the annexation of Panjdeh, he could not afford to dispense with Britain's patronage. Even so, he took good care to exclude from his kingdom, as far as possible, both British and Russian military and diplomatic representatives. He also secured the loyalty of his defeated Pathan tribal opponents by resettling them in non-Pathan areas, where their dislike of their neighbours would outweigh the temptation to rebel against a Pathan ruler.

The First World War, during which the Afghans, despite the many temptations, remained neutral as they had promised, deeply undermined the foundations of genuine imperial power for Britain; while, after 1917, the new communist régime in Russia was wholly absorbed in the problems of consolidating its domestic control. Thus the Afghans found themselves free to aspire to greater independence.

To some extent, independence was achieved as a reaction from the very restraint exercised by the Amir of Afghanistan during the war. Neutrality was exceedingly irksome to a people that saw in the war an opportunity to throw off the foreign yoke, and particularly that of the

British who ruled over parts of the old Afghan kingdom in the north-west of India. Moreover, there was always the excuse of going to the aid of the Caliph under attack from infidels – although such an excuse would have carried less weight in Afghanistan, rather isolated from the rest of the Muslim world, than in other Islamic countries. Hence, when Amir Habibullah was murdered in 1919, it was not difficult for his younger son Amanullah, darling of the hotheads and nationalists, and in control at the crucial moment of the key centre of Kabul, to seize power at the expense of his conservative elder brother. Amanullah, however, had an almost unlimited capacity for arousing the antagonism of the powerful conservative elements in the country, particularly the mullahs, the Muslim religious leaders. Within a very short time, he found his hold becoming precarious.

With considerable political astuteness, he launched, in May 1919, the third Afghan war with the British under the double pretext of a struggle for independence and a *Jihad,* or holy war. Although he was quickly defeated, his campaign achieved its objectives in a way that a rising between 1914–18 would have failed to do. This was the psychological moment. A war-weary, and wiser, Britain accorded full independence to Afghanistan by releasing it from all the limitations on its freedom of action in foreign affairs that had been imposed in the past. The Treaty of Rawalpindi of 1919 was followed by another in 1921 confirming the position. In the latter year, the Russians likewise signed a rather more grandiose, if less fully honoured, treaty. Amanullah was temporarily assured of his throne.

His retention of it, however, depended not on the British or the Russians but on his own people. The intemperate reforming zeal, probably stimulated by the reforms of Reza Shah in Persia, of a young man of limited ability, determined to drag his country into the twentieth century no matter how loud its protests, was too much for a society which was still living, quite contentedly, in the Middle Ages. Resistance to him took active shape in 1924, when he introduced a sweeping programme for the emancipation of women. This would not only have educated them but, even more provocative to traditionalists, would have freed them from complete domination by their menfolk. The mullahs raised the tribes in rebellion. One mullah was arrested for declaring the reforms to be against the law of Islam and for prophesying that 'when they come in, Islam will go out.' (This attitude still prevails today.) Although Amanullah's forces were eventually successful, the rebellion was brought to an end only when he agreed to allow the Loya Jirgah, the Great Assembly (a representative council of notables, not a body elected 'democratically' in the western sense), to repeal his measures. One cannot help wondering what became of those few women who went to Europe for education and were then called back to be reincarcerated in purdah.

Amanullah had neither the power nor the personality to create an acceptable system of modern government, greatly as this was needed. A country-wide trail of derelict and useless gadgetry, costing far more than Afghanistan's limited exchequer could bear, testified depressingly to the headlong and ill-informed way he had set about an essential task. He was encouraged to resume his reckless pursuit of wholesale reform and modernization when, late in 1927, he embarked on a splendid and extensive tour of Europe. Inspired by what he saw in more advanced countries, on his return in the following year he proclaimed again a programme of reforms. There was to be an assembly of one hundred and fifty elected representatives legislating and supervising the executive under a constitutional monarch; monogamy was to be introduced, along with compulsory and secularized education for children of both sexes. Implicit in his policy was the creation of separate 'church' and 'state' on the lines of the system developed (at the cost of much social and political strife) in some of the European countries he had visited. But such a policy, based on a distinction between the sacred and secular, and threatening as it did the power base and consequent material privileges of the mullahs, was quite incomprehensibly alien in an Islamic state at that time. All this he proclaimed to an assembly of chiefs and other notables, not made any more amenable by the enforced and embarrassing discomfort of surrendering their flowing tribal costume for European formal dress. Sir Francis Humphrys, British Minister in Kabul at the time, reported back of the King that

> He violated the safe conduct which he had given to the mullahs and tribal leaders by a series of open and clandestine executions; he banished out of jealousy for their influence with the people, the best brains and most experienced noblemen in the state; he allowed his inveterate hatred of the mullahs to pass all reasonable bounds; and finally he alienated the sympathies of his army by persistently ignoring their interests and by the importation of foreign advisers.[13]

Insurrection broke out again. This time, despite its unconcerted character, it continued with growing intensity until, in the ensuing disintegration of order and central authority, the throne in Kabul was seized by a Tajik brigand, Bachha-i-Saqao — 'son of the water carrier'. Amanullah himself retreated by stages to exile in Italy.

Thus, in 1929, it looked as if Afghanistan was about to

plunge yet again into one of its periods of anarchy. The Russians, who had been trying to exert influence at the Afghan court with only spasmodic success, were only too eager to exploit the situation. However, Britain, by declaring and following a policy of absolute neutrality in the struggle between the brigand usurper and his opponents, obliged Russia to do likewise. The internal struggle for power was undertaken by indigenous protagonists alone, and it soon transpired that the most effective of these was Nadir Khan, Amanullah's kinsman and founder of the last royal dynasty. His main strength lay in the support given him by tribes of the frontier districts. It is significant that Nadir owed his success as much to the tribes on the British side of the Durand Line – despite the efforts of the North-West Frontier Agency to prevent his recruiting there – as to those from the Afghan side. Early in October 1929, these forces took Kabul and on the sixteenth of the month Nadir was proclaimed King with the title of Muhammad Nadir Shah.

Nadir Shah was a man of sufficiently strong personality to attract the support of the tribes. Although at first he had to rely on these turbulent and unruly followers, he was able in the next four years, by identifying himself with the conservatives and by appointing his brothers to major ministerial posts, to stabilize the country. To ensure this stability, he and his successors built up the armed services in size, efficiency and prestige. The consequent potential for a military coup in a country where, apart from the tribes, there were no other organized power complexes, seems to have been overlooked. Nadir also reconstituted the Loya Jirgah, making it a body of delegates from every tribe and province. In 1930, after the confirmation of his accession, one hundred and five members were chosen – not of course, elected – to form a nucleus, meeting more regularly to rubber-stamp the decisions of the executive. Such was Nadir Shah's conservative concession to 'modernism', in contrast to Amanullah's sweepingly radical emulation of western institutions.

The new régime succeeded in diminishing the influence of the great powers by limiting their opportunities for operations of any kind in Afghanistan itself – whether diplomatic, military or economic – and by carefully balancing a concession to one by a concession to another. At the start of Nadir Shah's reign, the Russians crossed the Oxus into the virtually lawless northern provinces and penetrated deep into Afghan territory in pursuit of a bandit who had been harrassing the Russian side from an Afghan base and whom they thought the Afghans were too dilatory in bringing to justice. The incursion had the desired result of making the Afghans bring him to book themselves and, indeed, it accelerated the restoration of order and central control to the northern provinces. But soon Russian influence became as remote as British, and other Europeans – Germans in particular – began to play an increasing part in the technical development of Afghanistan.

When, four years after his succession, Nadir was assassinated by a schoolboy,* the transition of power to his son through a family regency was perfectly smooth. Throughout the 1930s, enjoying a considerable measure of internal stability, Afghanistan made its first serious steps towards economic development, particularly in communications, irrigation and the search for mineral resources. At the same time, its government refrained

---

*The youth was a natural son of Ghulam Nabi, executed by Nadir Shah as a prominent and disaffected adherent of Amanullah. But so isolated was the assassination from political action that it was certainly motivated by personal revenge, not political conspiracy.

from overvigorous expression of its dislike for the country's imperial neighbours. Though abating in no way its reluctance in practice to recognize the Durand Line as its southern frontier with the British empire in India, Afghanistan adhered to its declared neutrality throughout the Second World War. This neutrality was of critical importance in 1940 when Britain was stretched to its utmost and Germany was lavish in its blandishments in the hope that Afghanistan could be induced to create trouble on India's North-West Frontier.

As in 1919, a world war and its consequences were to have important repercussions for Afghanistan. The European imperial powers in Asia were everywhere in retreat after 1945. Their victory, the repossession of the lands lost to Japan and the retention of those they had successfully defended, was to be the farewell gesture of their power. Only in Soviet Asia were the imperialists not in retreat. Indeed, the German invasion of European Russia had accelerated the growth of industry and communications in Asiatic Russia where the Soviet authorities built up the economic 'masse de manœuvre' to defeat the Germans. While Britain's withdrawal from India in 1947 removed any remaining threat from Afghanistan's southern border, there was immediately beyond its northern border, a rapidly expanding economy and modern social organization among peoples ethnically akin to those on the Afghan side of the Oxus. To the west, only Britain's and America's expressed determination to use force if necessary had secured the withdrawal of a Russian army of occupation from northern Persia. This situation was in marked contrast to that among Afghanistan's neighbours and cousins to the south and east, among whom confusion reigned as a result of the bloody transfer of power, and who were in any case totally absorbed in the problems of trying to create a new state — Pakistan — out of nothing.

In many parts of Asia after the Second World War, the Americans tried to fill the vacuum left by the departure of the European powers. But for a variety of reasons, in the Indian subcontinent they could not adequately replace the bulwark of the British Empire against a downward thrust from Central Asia towards India. India itself gradually drifted from genuine neutrality in the 1950s into the pro-Soviet camp, largely as a reaction to US military support for the military régimes of an economically and politically unstable Pakistan. Twice the successor states to the Raj were at war, in 1965 and 1971, the second time with disastrous consequences for both the morale and the economic stability of West Pakistan. In the December 1970 elections which ended twelve years of military rule, Zulfiqar Ali Bhutto gained a clear majority in West Pakistan (but not, significantly, in Baluchistan or the North-West Frontier Province). However, Sheikh Mujibur Rahman's Awami league had swept the polls (90% of the popular vote) in East Pakistan. The Bangladesh, which had been a bazaar speculation for years, became a real possibility and when Rahman could not get the virtual autonomy he demanded, insurrection broke out in the eastern half of the divided nation. The largely western-recruited Pakistan army, a thousand miles from its supply base and compelled by a hostile India to fly round, not over, that country's territory, could not cope. In a last desperate attempt to relieve pressure in the east, Pakistan opened up the western front against India itself and within a fortnight the war was over, ninety thousand Pakistani prisoners were in Indian hands and some three thousand square miles of its former territory had been lost. The traumatic effect of this defeat still influences Pakistan's attitudes today and in particular its suspicion of America and reliance on China for military and economic assistance. (Conversely, the same mutual suspicion pushed Mrs Gandhi into a twenty-year pact with the Soviet Union.)

For the next five years, as a result of natural disasters, political dissension and economic mismanagement, Pakistan struggled unsuccessfully to tackle its problems − none of which were more significant for the future of the whole region than its clashes with neighbouring Afghanistan over the allegiance of the Pathans living within the borders of the new state. An understanding of this conflict, which has come to be known as the Pushtunistan issue, is essential to an appreciation of the Soviet Union's policy in Afghanistan and is the subject of the next chapter.

3 PUSHTUNISTAN UNJAST

'*Afghanistan Unjast, Pushtunistan Unjast! Afghanistan Unjast, Pushtunistan Unjast!*' Hour after hour the shrill, monotonous cry of the lorry-driver's *bacha** drove one slowly to the verge of frenzy on the long journey two decades ago, on the road from Kandahar to Kabul. 'This is Afghanistan, this is Pushtunistan!' It was as if a tourist on a motor coach drive down the Wye Valley from Monmouth to Chepstow were to find himself the captive audience of a fanatical Welsh Nationalist driver continually crying out 'Home Rule for Wales, Monmouthshire is Welsh!'

The Afghan slogan draws its inspiration from the Solomon-like arbitration of the colonial boundary draftsmen. In 1893, the British government in India, in an attempt to persuade the Amir of Afghanistan to restrain his Pathan subjects from their periodic descents on Her Majesty's subjects in her North-West Frontier Provinces, decided to establish a boundary commission to demarcate the frontiers between the Amir's and the Queen's

---

*One of these agile youths, whose prehensile powers are quite amazing, is to be found clinging to the back of most Afghan lorries. His chief function is to leap perilously between the wheels whenever the vehicle stops on a slope and to thrust behind them the large wooden wedge that does service for the long defunct brakes. He also helps the driver to collect the fares from the passengers. It is a kind of working apprenticeship.

dominions. After all, one could scarcely ask the Amir to restrain his subjects if he was uncertain as to who they were officially. Accordingly, Sir Mortimer Durand and his commission painstakingly delineated a frontier of military convenience, much of it running through the foothills which lead up to the Sulaiman mountains of Afghanistan itself. The 'convenient' frontier sliced through many tribal areas with an apparently bland disregard to ethnic affinities. This was matched by the steady disregard for British cartographical distinctions on the part of the people living along what came to be known as the Durand Line; they crossed from one side of it to another as if it did not exist, and were naturally indignant, in the usual forceful Pathan way, whenever they met with reprisals or obstructions for so doing. The restriction of an artificial frontier proved particularly irksome for nomads whose lives and movements were dictated by the location of traditional pastures from which they were now sometimes cut off.

While Amir Abdur Rahman, being a realist and bowing to superior force, accepted the Durand Line frontier, he did so grudgingly, for he was also a great patriotic leader and looked on all the Pathan areas as properly a part of his kingdom. In his autobiography Abdur Rahman declared that he did not regard the areas on the British side of the Durand Line as permanently ceded to the British, yet in that same volume he lists those very areas to which 'I renounce my claims.' Moreover, in the Treaty of Rawalpindi (1919), 'the Afghan government accepts the Indo-Afghan frontiers accepted by the late Emir.' The determination to regain these districts is a strong thread running through all subsequent Afghan history, and the opinion that they form a natural part of Afghanistan has been strongly held by all Afghanistan's recent rulers.

Lacking the relative strength which is the necessary ingredient of irredentism in the present climate of international opinion, Afghanistan has over the years modified its demand for the restoration of the old territory of the Durrani kingdom, superficially at least, to one for 'Pushtunistan': an independent state for the Pushtu-speaking peoples south and east of the Durand Line on the Pakistan side, Pushtu being the language of the Pathan tribesmen of both sides of this frontier. Such a state would naturally be expected to align itself closely with Afghanistan, but would not be a part of it. In the imagination of the Afghan cartographers, at least, this has already been accomplished, for the tourist guides issued to visitors clearly mark Pakistan's tribal territories as 'Pushtunistan'. What Afghanistan claims as Pushtunistan corresponds to the North-West Frontier Provinces of British India, the boundary of which ran from the border with China in the north to Baluchistan. (This latter area, it should be noted, is sometimes included in the proposed Pushtunistan.) It traverses every kind of scenery, from the great mountains and beautiful green valleys of Gilgit and Chitral to the Baluch desert — the dump, it is said, where Allah shot the rubbish of creation.

It is no marvel that this frontier should have been the setting of so many adventure stories of fifty or so years ago. Nature has conspired to create a backcloth appropriate to the character of the area's inhabitants. The scenic variety of the frontier districts on both sides of the Durand Line, indeed, seems almost unlimited. If you leave Kabul by the Lataband Pass as evening approaches, spiralling up the sinuous yellow road to nine thousand feet, you see the valley below and the hills around beginning to turn to a hard blue as the light fades. Then, as if nature is playing on a theatre organ, the sky's colour changes minute by minute. Just before the last streaks of purple, red and gold on the horizon darken into blackness, a storm breaks. There is no rain, and for a long time no thunder, and the lightning leaps nimbly from cloud to cloud showing up the mountain like a huge cardboard cutout. Here nature is so conscious of her power she disdains to bluster and threaten, and is content to dazzle. As you drive down the far side in the dark, the lightning projects a flickering photographic exhibition of small *chai khanas** revealed to their very depths, the lightning flashes so bright that the glowing lanterns on their verandahs are extinguished to the sight. Hills, trees and shrubs leap into momentary life, faces blink for a second and are shut in darkness again. Moving on down the Khyber at dawn to Peshawar, you leave behind the narrow defile speckled with innumerable plaques commemorating the otherwise forgotten deeds of heroism of those who fought to take and hold the pass.

Turning around at neatly geometrical, Raj-redolent Peshawar, your road leads south and west again, this time on the Pakistan side of the frontier, until you reach Kohat where a local restaurateur pounces to lead you to the heart of the town. You are being conducted to the sanctum of a master magician, past the booths of lesser conjurors and quacks – only the magic on this occasion is solely culinary. Don't close your eyes in passing each stall or you may succumb to the temptation of their many smells: roasting corn cobs, nuts and a variety of meats. With your eyes open the temptation will not

---

Chai khanas are the tea-houses which, in non-alcoholic Afghanistan, are the nearest equivalent to the Englishman's pub – or, rather, to the Irishman's or the Covent Garden porter's pubs, which are open pretty well all the time.

seduce you, for their living coat of bulge-headed flies is enough to deter all but a starving or a Pathan stomach. The magician's cave itself is plunged in gloom, and against this background the long-bearded patron crouches over a row of gleaming bowls that catch the light prying through the open side of the shop. Raised on his dais, he deigns to give you a welcoming nod then, prince of devils, returns to gloat over and stir the vegetable afrits in his explosive cauldrons. A strong smell of spice hangs over them as they cook, although 'cook' is a tame word to describe the process, for gouts of yellow liquid leap like shell splashes round the bright red tomatoes which eddy round lower in the bowl, while rich green chilis, newly added, slip furtively between them.

Continuing your journey beyond Kohat, you are treated to a geological extravaganza. The road plunges into a crazy, Neapolitan ice of clay and red and yellow sandstone. The whole terrain has in many places been tilted through ninety degrees by the earth's movement, and yet the different strata are still sharply defined. Much of the softer layers has been worn away, leaving sharp fins of harder rock only a few feet thick but miles long and hundreds of feet high. The space between is occasionally cultivated, but more often it is just a bare hot strip of dust. From there you come to a region of harder rocks cut with gorges and passes, the road clinging to the lip of a ravine hundreds of feet above a marble-green river. Out of one pillar of rock a huge head, a hybrid of Greek and Asiatic, has been carved. From time to time you emerge from the gullies through the hills on to stretches of flat desert, or semi-desert, gravel and small stones, often crossed by wide, shallow watercourses left by the year's rain, which seems to fall in a wasteful few days and swiftly disappear. At one point, the desert is broken by an incongruous ten-mile belt of cultivated jungle, after which it changes its nature yet again. The scenery is startlingly evocative of one of Hollywood's fanciful films about the Foreign Legion. The desert, with its outcrops of honeycombed sandstone, high temperature and Colorado atmosphere, is dotted with 'legion' forts, manned by the North-West Frontier Force. The desert is the home of a multitude of dust demons: spirals of sand thirty to a hundred feet high which swirl tortuously across the landscape, elastically changing shape as they go.

You may spend the night at one of the garrisons where the officers' mess seems more Sandhurst than Sandhurst, but where the entertainment is essentially Pathan: a display perhaps of tribal dancing and satire. The dance is rather like the Afghan *atan,* the dancers hopping about like birds and jerking their heads sharply from side to side, thus making a flying plumage of their long black hair. The music is without melody, the rhythm varying greatly, the dancers coming at moments almost to a standstill and at others jumping and stamping in a sforzando of frenzy punctuated by regular crashing breaks. The musicians, four in number, walk slowly round inside the circle of dancers, clapping on small tabors or playing on a wailing reed instrument. The purpose of the dance is to excite a battle frenzy; erotic dances, common to western cultures, play but a small part in these predominantly male societies. By the glazed look of some of the dancers after forty minutes, the desired result seems to be achieved. The dance is followed by a pantomime which gives full scope to the Pathan's great gift for mimicry and comic gesture, and in which the ordinary soldier seizes the opportunity to satirize his officers.

The journey gets harder as you drive on south-west, this time in the cab of a bus bursting at the rivets with passengers; there are twelve in the driver's cab alone. The floor is heaped up with baskets; jammed tightly against them, you prop your feet on a stone water-jar, knees pushed up to the chin so that you can scarcely move in any direction and are forced into the meditative position of a more than usually masochistic fakir. Your clothes stick in clammy swabs to those of your neighbours and mutual sweats mingle in one steady flow. On one side of you is a man with 'flu and on the other his pock-faced son who leans his head on your shoulder and sprawls over your legs. A third, clad in a loud check shirt is jabbering and spitting like a human monkey, and all over you crawl two small children whose lips and faces are burst open by suppurating boils and festering sores. The heat, sweat, noise and stench is such that even the acrid smell of *biri*, the rolled tobacco leaves that make up a Pakistani cigarette, is a welcome anaesthetic.

At last you reach Dalbandin, the town everyone has been talking about in the bus. You feel an immense relief, but when you clamber out you realize that Dalbandin is only a small group of huts around a few government offices, a fort and a railway station: a mere village surviving in a wilderness of sand that assaults it in tireless waves which appear to be sucking up its outposts inch by inch. Yet there is a gaunt beauty in its few blasted trees waving desperate, crazy fingers out of their graves of sand and in the simplicity of its white-fronted buildings defying the desert. On one edge of the village, next to the football pitch – just a patch of sand a little less soft than the rest – you find a resthouse that has somehow snatched a comparative paradise from the ground of this desert hell. There is a pool in the compound, and grass, and green trees, and clumps of a lovely bush which blossoms with warm pink and orange flowers.

On again, this time in the single-track train that runs like a lifeline through the Pakistan frontier provinces and Baluchistan. You are now out of the territories of the Pathans proper and well into Baluchistan. Here

The desert singes, and the stubborn rock
Split to the centre sweats at every pore.[1]

Your nostrils are suddenly assailed by the pungent odour of the earth's flesh on fire, scorching beneath the sun as unmistakably as that of any human body. For over two hundred miles there is no water at all except that brought once a week in the wagons of the train. Nor is there any natural wild life except the 'sandfish': a small snake-like creature about the size of a blindworm and of a light sandy colour. There is nothing apparently for it to live on, yet it survives, and from its tail the natives extract a precious oil used in the making of perfume. Villages here exist only because of the treasures of the desert and the black hot hills that traverse it: manganese and other minerals or, as at Nok Kundi, the most beautiful marble in Asia. Perfume and marble; Eve's beauty from the serpent's tail and palaces quarried and fetched from the very mouth of hell.

It is these varied territories and differing peoples of the southern frontier districts which the Afghan government dreams of making into a single coherent state. The lorry-driver's *bacha* should be calling, not *'Pushtunistan Unjast,'* but *'Pushtunistan Kujast?'* − 'Where is Pushtunistan?'

Apart from the sentimental attachments of the royal family, a mixture of gratitude and fear probably provided a subconscious motive for the desire of Afghanistan's autocratic monarchs over the past forty years to see the Pathan areas as a whole come within a greater degree of Afghan control, however theoretically indirect. During the chaos that followed Amanullah's overthrow in 1929, the British carefully refrained from any involvement and, verbally at least, tried to disassociate the tribesmen on their side of the frontier from the subsequent struggle for power in Afghanistan. These British admonitions, however, were ineffective, and the bulk of the tribal forces which gave Nadir Shah the ultimate victory were, in fact, recruited south of the Durand Line.

Immediately after World War Two the Afghans were keenly quoting every British opinion which by any stretch of the imagination could be said to uphold the validity of their claim for an independent Pushtunistan in the new India. It must be remembered that at this time the constitutional plan at least envisaged that many of the Princely States would retain their autonomy, not that they would be militarily annexed by the 'pacifist' government of India. The Bray Committee's view that 'if self-determination is to be allowed any play at all in India, it should surely be allowed to the Pathan race, whom providence has interposed between India and foreign aggression',[2] was music to Afghan ears and from Mountbatten's remark that 'agreements with the tribes on the North-West Frontiers of India would have to be negotiated with the appropriate successor authority'[3] they inferred that he favoured their claim. In my view he referred to internal agreements between the tribes and what subsequently became Pakistan. The last Viceroy made it quite clear that in his role as referee he could take no stance, but that it was for the two parties involved in the partition of India, Congress and the

Muslim League, to decide whether or not the frontier would be an independent state. The British government in India in 1944 in fact sharply reminded the Afghans that the Durand Line was an established international boundary which should not concern them. The referendum conducted in the North-West Frontier Province in 1947 thus offered the Pathans south-east of the Durand Line only the choice of joining India or Pakistan, a limitation about which the Afghans, with some justice, complained. Abdul Ghaffar Khan — the frontier Gandhi — and his brother campaigned hard for the boycott of the referendum, but had little impact as the 55% poll was only some 10% down on previous polling levels. Inevitably 99% of those voting opted for Pakistan and it became the position of the British government at independence, and has been since, that Pakistan became legal heir to all the treaty rights secured by the British in India.

The division of the Pathan tribes by the Durand Line led, after the partition of the Indian subcontinent in 1947, to an uneasy relationship between Afghanistan and Pakistan. The Afghans felt that their ambitions were now opposed by a weaker force; the Pakistanis, acutely conscious of their problems in welding together a new state from so many disparate entities, were determined that nothing should detract from strengthening the sense of national unity. Inevitably the two countries came to loggerheads over Pushtunistan.

In 1949 Pakistan air force planes operating on the frontier accidentally bombed a village on the Afghan side. Pakistan apologized and offered compensation. Afghanistan rejected all overtures and the Afghan Shura — then appointed by the King, not elected — proclaimed that it recognized 'neither the imaginary Durand nor any similar Line.' In a speech at that time the King, Zahir

Shah, used a significant phrase. 'Note also must be taken of the freedom-loving aspirations and the repeated protests of the trans-Durand *Afghans*. . . . '

The Afghan authorities encouraged the setting up of a so-called independent Pakhtun parliament in Pakistan itself. The Pakistanis responded by cutting off transit fuel supplies to Afghanistan and broadcasting demands to know whether Afghanistan proposed to grant independence to the Pathans on their side of the frontier − a challenge always calculated to provoke the fury of Afghan governments. On a more positive note, the Pakistan government made great efforts to make the tribes feel that they belonged to Pakistan and that their citizenship brought substantial material benefits. As a deliberate act of policy, expenditure in the tribal areas on education, health and rural development has been disproportionately high in relation to expenditure on these things in other parts of Pakistan. Conversely, the transfer from tribal law and customs to the rule of national law has been tactfully gradual. A steady recruitment of men from the tribal areas to the Pakistan regular army − among whose élite troops such North-West Frontier Forces as the Waziristan Scouts stand supreme − also serves to increase their attachment to Pakistan. When they are released from military service to return to their villages, they take with them not only the skills and literacy, but also the attitudes that they have acquired in the army. It is perhaps significant that in many villages it is still regarded as a matter of honour to furnish the local quota of men for military service.

Over the next ten years the dispute fluctuated in intensity, though, as my experience recounted at the beginning of this chapter indicates, it remained an active myth in the popular mind and a useful rallying cry on the domestic political scene on both sides of the frontier.

In 1960, however, it once again brought the two neighbours to the brink of outright war.

Diplomatic relations between Afghanistan and Pakistan had been resumed in 1957, after a two-year lapse following the merger of all the Western States of Pakistan, including the North-West Frontier Province, into a single West Pakistan. But, at the end of 1959, Pakistan felt compelled to protest against violations of its air space by Afghan aircraft and against provocative broadcasts on Kabul radio by the King and Premier in which both, in the name of Pushtunistan, repeated earlier claims to parts of Pakistan. These incidents were the culmination of a persistent and increasingly tough attitude fostered by Daoud over the Pushtunistan question. In March 1960, Khrushchev publicly supported the Afghan claims. Pakistan riposted by proposing a referendum among Afghan Pathans to see if they would like to join Pakistan. The Afghans retorted by refusing to extend the visas of Pakistanis working in their country, expelling a number of them and making the life of those who remained virtually impossible. Pro-Pushtunistan propaganda was intensified by Afghan consular agencies, whose activities in this field had already aroused deep indignation in Pakistan.

It is difficult to decide exactly who started the fighting which broke out in the Bajaur area, north of the Khyber Pass, in September 1960 and again in May 1961. Pakistan claimed that it was repulsing incursions into its territory by armed groups backed by the Afghan army. The Afghans counter-claimed that Pakistan was in fact conducting a severe campaign of military reprisals and bombing against discontented Pathan tribesmen within its own borders. The Pakistanis admitted the bombing of one house, which they said was the headquarters of Afghan agents.

Afghan regular troops disguised as tribesmen were badly defeated by local Frontier Force soldiers and local villagers, but Punjabi units sent in by Ayub Khan, Pakistan's Pathan president, to support the local forces, received a scarcely less hostile reception. Apportioning blame in an area where the movements of population are considerable is not easy, although personally I feel that Pakistan probably had slightly the better case. Whatever the origins of the conflict, diplomatic relations were broken off in September 1961 and frontier traffic came to a standstill. By November, something like two hundred thousand Afghan nomads, who habitually leave their summer pastures in Afghanistan for winter work in Pakistan, found themselves stranded and near starvation in the mountain passes between the two countries, although a few managed to force their way over the border. The closure of the frontier was a sharp blow to the Afghan economy, and its consequences contributed to the resignation in March 1963, after ten years as virtual ruler of Afghanistan, of Prince Daoud. With Daoud gone, tension between the two countries began to ease and, through the good offices of the Shah of Persia, diplomatic relations were restored in May. Feelings remained strong, however, and in 1966, Maiwandwal, then Prime Minister of Afghanistan, made it quite clear in conversation with me that he thought the Pushtunistan issue as serious then as ever – perhaps even more serious, in that despite the expressed regret of both sides over the clash in 1960–61, there had been complete failure to resolve the dispute to the satisfaction of all three parties: Pakistan, Afghanistan and the Pathans.

Thus, in its seemingly inevitable decennial cycle, the issue came to a head again in the mid-1970s. This time the problem was aggravated by two additional factors: increasing demands for greater regional independence in Pakistan and growing fears of the central Pakistan government that these might lead to the further disintegration of the state. The secession of East Pakistan to become the sovereign state of Bangladesh has made subsequent Pakistan governments, whether civilian or military, almost paranoid about any hint of further separatism. Though Bhutto's 1970 election victory was overwhelming in the rest of Pakistan, he was badly defeated in the NWFP and in Baluchistan he did not even win a single seat. The bulk of popular support was clearly for those parties, such as the National Awami Party, favouring if not outright independence, a very high degree of regional autonomy. In order to contain these fissiparous pressures, the 1973 constitution devolved considerable federal powers to the regional governments which had been created in 1970. In response to local demand, there was also substantial investment in transport, medical services and education in these two regions, within the limit permissible in the precarious state of Pakistan's economy. The stabilizing effect of such measures was, however, diminished by the sudden return to power in Afghanistan of that ardent irredentist Daoud. Within a few days of taking over he was stirring up the old Pushtunistan issue which had played so large a part in his downfall a decade earlier. Though initially he spoke of 'a peaceful and honourable settlement of the Pushtunistan problem' and 'the hopes of the Baluch people', it was soon evident that his demands, and the tactics by which they were pursued, were no different from those of the late 1950s and early 1960s.

By 1975 Pakistan was bitterly, and on good evidence, accusing Afghanistan of stirring up trouble on the Pakistan side of the frontier, trouble which culminated in the assassination of H.M.K. Sherpao, a leading opponent of Pushtunistan in the NWFP government. The Pakistan Defence Minister denounced Afghanistan for training guerillas, mounting sabotage and assassinations in Pakistan and for harbouring 'absconders from justice'. His view that the 'sole aim of these activities is to create unrest and fear amongst the people of the NWFP and Baluchistan in advancement of Afghanistan's aggressive and irredentist aims' is hard to deny.

In February that year, governor's rule was imposed in the NWFP as it was in Baluchistan in December, the National Awami Party was dissolved and its leader Wali Khan arrested — in effect for preaching the supreme heresy, secession.

General Zia's military coup in 1976 and ensuing events in Afghanistan itself, slightly lowered the temperature, but the fact that once again the tribal areas south of the Durand Line are being used by rebels against a Kabul régime to try to topple it by military means, makes the situation more potentially dangerous than it has been at any time in this century. To measure these risks it is necessary to examine the validity of the moral, social and psychological basis of Afghanistan's Pushtunistan claims, rather than their, in my view, shaky legal foundations. The basis of the Afghan claim is that the Pushtu-speaking peoples are an artifically divided ethnic entity. That they are of the same race on both sides of the Durand Line cannot be in dispute, but that this border is the artificial and sole cause of division is open to argument. It is fallacious to assume that the Pathans are a naturally homogeneous whole. Their entire history is, rather, one of fierce and cruelly conducted intertribal disputes over everything from grazing grounds to kingdoms. Great tribes like the Yusufzai and the Durrani have been continually at skirmish with each other for centuries, and feelings of deep antagonism remain.

The essential characteristic of the Pathan tribe is a closely knit and sharply defined pattern of family relationships that places everyone not of that group, and quite irrespective of his ethnic origins, among the world of potential enemies. At the same time, the Pathan – of whatever tribe – has a strong pride in being a Pathan. The tribal group is the limit of the extent to which the Pathan is prepared to abate his jealously guarded individualism. Even within the family circle, rivalries and quarrels are often long and bitter, since the Pathan calls no man lord and admits his inferiority to nobody. To the world outside his tribal group, and apart from the demands of hospitality to wayfaring strangers, the Pathan's attitude alternates between a total indifference and a kind of tigerish contempt for the rest of the human animal kingdom, whose function is to provide, when necessary, individuals to satisfy the predator's appetite. Mountstuart Elphinstone, a most penetrating observer of Afghan life, graphically describes the character of the Pathan in his *Account of the Kingdom of Caubul.*

> Their vices are revenge, envy, avarice, rapacity and obstinacy; on the other hand, they are fond of liberty, faithful to their friends, kind to their dependants, hospitable, brave, hardy, frugal, laborious and prudent; they are less disposed than the nations in their neighbourhood to falsehood, intrigue and deceit.[4]

The Pathan character has changed little since the year 1814, when Elphinstone completed his account. Gun-carrying is no longer mandatory, nor failure to go armed a case of being improperly dressed; but one man in four still carries rifle, shotgun or pistol, and those that no longer go gun in hand still have one at home – just in case. Gaily decorated, near-perfect handmade imitations of the classic weapons of every nation are manufactured at the tribal arms factory near Kohat in Pakistan; examples can be seen bristling from the top of every market-bound bus or lorry. The occasional ornate *jezail* (one of those ancient muskets which seem more likely to destroy their owners than their targets) or the intricately decorated sheath of a triangular-bladed hunting-knife, evoke memories of the stirring adventures vividly narrated by writers of the Henty school and hardly less vividly re-enacted by many a British schoolboy in his back garden.

Generosity and nobility of manner can yield to the most scathingly expressed form of contempt in the world: an ice-basilisk glance and a tiny gobbet of precision-planted spit at the despised one's feet. Moving with a springing stride, toes turned slightly inwards and rising at the heel, and with a tall, haughty carriage, the Pathan will flash at you from beneath stern black eyebrows a fierce look that can turn suddenly into a shy glance of soft brown eyes. Warlike spirit shares his soul with childish and delightful vanity, and a Pathan will lay down his rifle and cartridge belt, sit on a little peninsula of stones by the stream and pluck, paint and preen himself with more than a woman's vanity in the mirror-shine of the lid of a boot-polish tin. A courteous and unembarrassed 'good day' from him, striding past you as you attend to the call of nature in the desert; the care and protection of you, his guest, as an unquestioned obligation, even to death; his manly independence; his Rabelaisian humour – all this makes the Pathan a man to be liked and respected, to be treated tactfully and carefully; and a man rarely, if ever, to be organized within the impersonal conventions of a modern state.

It is highly unlikely that people of such a prickly and individualistic temperament, inheriting many intertribal enmities, antipathetic to the very idea of central rule, are going to agitate very forcefully for the creation of Pushtunistan – unless such agitation can serve as a means for satisfying their, until recently, much thwarted lust for a good fight. Their outlook is, after all, little different now from the days when the Pushtu poet, Khushal Khan, trying vainly to unite the tribes against the Mogul Emperor Aurangzebe, bewailed: 'Would that the Pushtuns could agree among themselves.'

The real weakness of Afghan claims, to those more concerned with justice than law, lies in their lack of logical coherence, their internal contradictions. During an amiable, lengthy and courteous interview with me in 1966, Prime Minister Maiwandwal for just one brief instant sparked a flash of anger; it was when I asked him whether he thought any part of Afghanistan should become part of Pushtunistan. His sharp 'never' and subsequent rebuke of my 'irrelevant' question betrayed, not only strength of feeling, but perhaps also an awareness of the ambiguity and weakness of the arguments for an independent Pushtunistan. If there is a case to be made out for Pushtunistan on the grounds of natural ethnic affinity, assessed in terms of language, then all Pushtu-speaking peoples, from both sides of the border, should belong to it; which means that it should be created from territories belonging to Afghanistan no less than to Pakistan. If this case falls, partial groupings cutting across established states and boundaries make no sense in terms of securing stable and equitable territorial demarcation in this part of Asia. It may, however, seem to make sense in terms of other considerations. We shall see later, from the attitude of the Pathan ruling group in Afghanistan towards the minorities there, that the assumption by this group that

Afghanistan is already a natural Pathan state has at least as much, and maybe more, significance for internal as for external interests.

One should not expect those involved to apply pure logic to the argument, in public at least. Pushtunistan, like the reunification of Germany, is one of those causes that no national leader or politician dare renounce, however little faith he may himself have in it; the cause has its own logic. Yet danger lies in an issue which, kept simmering for a variety of reasons, can suddenly be brought to the boil whenever the Soviet Union chooses to apply more intense heat to the pot. It is an established axiom of Russian policy that the Durand Line was part of a wicked imperialist plot which it was Afghanistan's duty to overthrow. In August 1951, for example, an article in *Literaturnaya Gazeta* declared:

> As a direct result of the enforced division of the Afghan tribes, who are almost equally divided between Afghanistan and Pakistan and are carrying on a struggle for self-determination, and also as a result of the original traditions of the numerous nomad tribes, a situation is arising apparently of itself, apparently spontaneously, in which there could occur demarcation by bloodshed of the frontier that was originally plotted on the maps of the imperialists in London and [*sic!*] Washington. Spontaneously rising tension, mutual enmity and incidents are exactly what the imperialists need in order to divide and rule.

It so happened that 'tension' and the rest were also exactly what the Soviet imperialist philosophy of that time needed to facilitate its territorial expansion. But after the clash of 1960–61 between Afghanistan and Pakistan, the Russian attitude changed. Having made a notable effort in 1965–66 to compose the quarrel between India and Pakistan over Kashmir, Russia did not want to see yet another frontier war flaring up in an area where the development of its interests required stability. Moscow seemed to recognize that such divisions in the Indian subcontinent were of benefit only to Peking. The main aim of Soviet diplomatic effort was to persuade Afghanistan and Pakistan that they had mutual economic interests, for it was on this recognition that the unhampered flow of her own goods through these countries largely depended.

Although Afghan governments often include Baluchistan in the proposed Pushtunistan, the Baluch are not of the same stock and are no more fond of the Pathans than are the other minorities they dominate. The presence of some million Pathans in Pakistan Baluchistan itself, does not improve the relationship. In demographic terms the issue is of minor importance to Afghanistan, as only a very small proportion, probably no more than one hundred thousand to two hundred thousand of the two million plus Baluch live, or wander, on the Afghan side of the border. The majority live either in Pakistan or in the south-east corner of Iran where, as Sunni Muslims, they constitute an ill-regarded religious minority.

Baluchistan, however, for all the hostile aspect of its largely uninhabited desert (see map on page 79) has a number of highly desirable economic features. The Sui gasfields have already begun to be exploited, but there are also considerable deposits of chrome, sulphur, coal and iron ore which have not yet been developed and it possesses that economic holy grail of Russian imperialism − access to the warm waters of the Arabian Sea. It is thus a desirable territory not only for its present rulers, Pakistan, and its covetous neighbour, but for the Soviet Union. Nor could a stable and strong Iran afford to ignore its fate, as the Shah indicated in 1972 when he implied that in the event of the collapse of Pakistan he would occupy Baluchistan. In December 1979 sharp fighting with considerable casualties was reported from Iranian Baluchistan, when the regional capital Zahedan tried to assert its independence of Teheran.

The Baluch, however, are still largely a primitive, unsophisticated, and in many cases nomadic people, who do not have sufficient skilled citizens to exploit their hard to develop economic potential on their own. They do have a strong desire for a greater degree of control over their own destiny and bitterly resent the fact that their fierce opposition to central government has three times been bloodily suppressed by military force in this decade. Political activity is in any case banned throughout Pakistan by President Zia, but perhaps more significant than the absence of a political outlet is the fact that early in 1979 the National Awami Party, which had expressed the desire for autonomy of both the Pathans and the Baluch, split into two wings. The division was on racial and political lines with the Pakistani Pathans adopting a more moderate less separatist stance, while the Baluch moved still further to the left.* The Baluch position was largely dictated by the fact that a number of its young men had been to Russia in recent years for training and had returned ardent Marxist revolutionaries. They had, for example, greeted the Taraki coup in Afghanistan with delight as a step nearer their own independence. Their no less nationalist elders, however, as orthodox Muslims, were much less enthusiastic. Many of them are realistic enough to recognize that they would find it almost impossible to survive alone — even if any new independent state of Balu-

---

*It is well to remember that whenever referring to Afghan Marxists in this part of the world, we are always dealing in terms of very small numbers.

chistan were to embrace the Baluch in all three countries. But unless those three countries can gratify the economic and political desires of the Baluch, the temptation offered by Soviet client-state status may prove considerable as the Moscow-indoctrinated young men move up into positions of power. Though the immediate prospects of fostering effective revolt and secession are less in Baluchistan than in Pushtunistan, the gains, from the Soviet point of view, are much more attractive. An independent, Soviet-dominated Baluchistan would sit astride the entrance to the Iranian Gulf as well as opening up the Arabian Sea for the direct outward flow of Russian goods.

If the classical concept of Afghanistan as a buffer state had held true in the post-war world, Russia might have been expected to move in as soon as the counter-pressure of the British Empire was removed. That it did not, was a clear indication that the policy makers in the Kremlin believed that they were moving successfully at second hand towards their economic and political goals in the region. So what kind of society were they trying to manage, and how did they succeed in penetrating it so thoroughly?

4 WHO ARE THE AFGHANS?

Though often the most dramatic, relations with other countries are not the most critical of Afghanistan's problems. The real tasks facing its governments are internal: the problem of unity and minorities; the conflicting pressures, social and economic, of traditionalism and modernization (particularly in regard to the status of women and to Islam); and the difficulties of imposing sophisticated political methods and institutions on old tribal loyalties and attitudes. In subsequent chapters, we shall examine political developments in Afghanistan in recent years and assess the country's economic resources and the attempts made to harness them. Here we shall trace the main features of Afghan society and try to explain the factors that have conditioned its political and economic development.

The most challenging of the problems facing Afghanistan is the creation of a sense of genuine national unity in a country whose constituent races have as little natural affinity as had those of Britain before and immediately after the Norman Conquest. When most foreigners use the word 'Afghan' they are usually thinking of the Pathans, forgetting that among the country's inhabitants are very substantial minorities of Uzbegs, Hazaras, Turkmen and Tajiks, not to speak of many smaller groups, such as Aimaq, Kirghiz and Nuristani.

A reasonably accurate population survey carried out

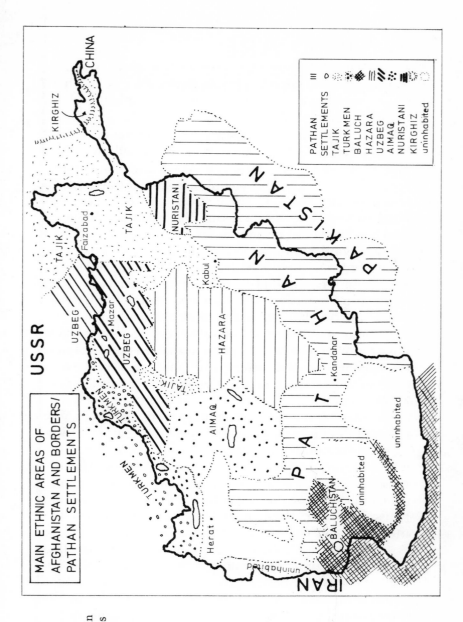

Map 3: Main racial groups

by AID in 1973 gave the settled population as a little over ten million, growing at just under 2% a year. There were probably a further two million nomads, whose numbers remain fairly constant.

Dupree, on whose work the ethnic map on page 79 is based, made a 1973 estimate of fourteen million (a little high in my view). A 1978 Afghan government survey using AID based data and techniques gave a figure of fifteen and a half million, which also seems high. These official surveys avoided breaking the numbers down by race for political reasons. Estimates of the number of Pathans vary from Dupree's 50% to 75%. The most likely figure seems to be between 50% and 60%. The largest minority is that of the Tajiks at between three and four million. Then there are about a million Uzbegs, and a million Hazaras, and almost as many Aimaq and Nuristanis, before we come down to the innumerable minor groups. Overall the present figure is probably between fourteen and fifteen million. The World Bank team in 1977 suggested that a population explosion may be imminent.

Though the main races dominate particular areas, as a result of calculated policies of dispersal by various rulers in the twentieth century, there are pockets of racially different settlements in these main regions. Usually these consist of Pathans in non-Pathan areas. A significant indication of the respective status of the different races is that in these mixed areas while Pathan immigrant males quite often marry local girls, the reverse is seldom true. A glance at the map will also show that with the exception of the almost psychotically independent Hazaras and Nuristanis, all the main racial groups in Afghanistan are part of ethnic areas which straddle the Afghan border — a fact as likely to be significant to that country's future as it has been in the past.

The picture is further complicated by the existence and movement of the main nomad groups in the southeast, in Baluchistan, and in Badakshan in the north. By far the largest and most important of these groups is the Ghilzai, the most numerous of the true Afghan tribes, and with a reputation among foreigners for fanaticism and savagery unequalled even in Afghanistan. At one time the Ghilzai (or Ghalji) conquered much of Persia.

The nomads play a major function in the commercial and financial life of the villages on their route, often bringing and selling goods, lending money and even owning land and collecting rent. They also serve as an uncontrollable (and therefore in Kabul eyes unacceptable) means of disseminating news of what is happening in other parts of the country. Increasingly often in recent years, they have either found their communal grazing land permanently occupied by pioneering farmers backed by the army, or barred to them by the political closure of frontiers they had never recognized. Perhaps not surprisingly the nomads look on the farmers with contempt, but it is they that always have to find an alternative grazing area.

While placing great official emphasis on the need for national unity, successive governments of Afghanistan have done little to foster it in practice. Prime Minister Maiwandwal, for example, optimistically declared to me in 1966: 'We do not think in terms of ethnic entities. We consider everybody in Afghanistan as Afghans.' This was an admirable goal at which to strive, but even now most of the minority groups would not agree that it was being achieved. No democratic administration has ever had more than two non-Pathans in any cabinet, though these have usually numbered from fifteen to twenty people. Dr Yusuf's in 1963, for example, had none. Nor has that even larger underprivileged group, women, who form about 55% of the population of Afghanistan, been even as well represented as that. There have only ever been three women in the cabinet, never more than one at a time, and never in any post except the health and social welfare field thought appropriate to them. President Karmal's February 1980 cabinet did contain four non-Pathans (out of sixteen) but this is not so surprising in view of the fact that the revolutionary cause was bound to attract support from among the minority groups who resented the apparently perpetual Pathan dominance. His cabinet has only one woman in it, his mistress Dr Ratebzad. The minorities have always felt that Afghanistan is a country run by Pathans for Pathans and that the other groups are, in a sense, the victims of an internal colonialism. This is an impression which must be shared by the foreign visitor. It is strengthened by past governments' preoccupation with exclusively Pathan issues, such as Pushtunistan, the status and use of Pushtu and the dominance of the 'Pathan' capital, Kabul. Gestures, such as making Turki an offical language, did little to convince the minorities otherwise. A form of Persian known as Dari is the language common to the Afghan ethnic groups (not necessarily as the first language), except that many uneducated Pathans speak only Pushtu.

The government of this volatile mixture is firmly in the hands of the Pathans. You will find Pathan governors in most of the provinces, even where the population is predominantly of another ethnic group, but not — partly, it is true, because of the problem of the Pushtu language — a non-Pathan governor of a Pathan province. The overwhelming majority of administrators are also Pathans. In fairness, it must be said that the Pathans have a flair for administration and that even in an openly competitive society, without ethnic bias, they would probably come out with more than their share, relative to their proportion of the population, of key government and administrative posts.

The favoured position of the Pathans in modern Afghanistan is symbolized by the way in which Kabul thrives, apparently at the expense of the provinces. In amenities and services, Kabul is to a great extent a typical modern metropolis. New blocks of offices and houses are springing up among the old mud dwellings; cars, restaurants and well-stocked shops abound, as one would expect in a capital city. But its array of amenities and services is out of proportion when the city's three-quarter million population is compared with that of the whole country.

For example, some 80% of Afghanistan's sorely needed doctors practise in Kabul, where the prospects of augmenting their meagre government salaries by private practice are best, and where there are hospital facilities. This gives Kabul a ratio of about one doctor per thousand people, as opposed to a national figure of one per thirteen thousand. I have been in remote northern districts where the doctor had two hundred thousand patients on his list, no hospital, no assistants, no nurses and not even a local dispensary for drugs. His was the only car in the district and he worked for little better than a skilled labourer's wage. Sixty percent of the 2,700 hospital beds are in the capital, which also enjoys the same proportion of the country's domestic electricity supply and piped water. Similarly with education; the capital has almost a monopoly of the best facilities. Almost all institutions of higher education, universities and technical colleges are at present centred in Kabul, although in the past decade they have been extended to Jalalabad, Herat, Kunduz and Mazar, and the technical college in Kandahar has grown considerably. A student who has once been to Kabul does everything in his power, or more often in his family's power, to avoid being sent back to the provinces. This is particularly true of the few women students. The provinces are thus deprived of the very people needed to demand and create the missing amenities and services, and so the vicious circle continues.

While it is true that members of other ethnic groups in Kabul do benefit from its growth, the capital is essentially a Pathan-dominated city, and its growing modernity is viewed with envy by the provincial Uzbeg or Hazara. As yet, few of these are sufficiently educated to appreciate the extent of the imbalance and to turn their resentment into any more active protest.

Some improvements have also taken place in the provinces. But even these are concentrated in the Pathan areas to the south and south-east of the Hindu Kush. The great schemes of agricultural development in Khost and the Helmand Valley, of forestry at Ali Khel, of hydro-electric power and agricultural irrigation in Nangarhar — these are all in Pathan provinces; and even where development is taking place in regions where other groups predominate, as with cotton ginning and processing in the north, at Kundųz and along the Oxus, it is often in an area with a Pathan settler population dating from the government's deliberate shifting of Pathans to these areas before the Second World War.

In the main, the Pathans live south of the great barrier of the Hindu Kush, and the bulk of the minority groups live to its north or in the south-west. Until the Salang Tunnel was opened in 1964, the mountains to all intents and purposes, in winter at least, sealed off one half of the country from the other. Over the last few years, communications between Kabul and the main provincial cities have improved considerably, both by road and air, although such important centres as Faizabad and Farah are still linked to the capital by dirt roads whose monstrous potholes and fist-sized stones prove the best free breaker's yard in the world for any car. Communications between the provinces themselves are virtually non-existent. To travel between Mazar-i-Sharif and Kunduz – the capital of the important neighbouring province of that name – you take your choice of the various tyre tracks of those who have passed across the desert before, and at the same time try to follow the meandering line of dilapidated wooden beanposts bearing the single telephone line. To reach Kunduz from some of its outlying districts, you must cross the river by a wooden ferry whose ballast system, a masterpiece of ingenious simplicity, consists of bailing water from one of the two hulls, side by side catamaran style, to its equally rickety partner, while motive power is achieved by hauling on a rope. The one hundred and eighty kilometre journey between the two towns can take nine or ten hours' driving, with time off for digging two-wheel-drive vehicles out of the sand. There is not likely to be more than a single vehicle travelling in the opposite direction – which in these narrow switchback tracks is just as well.

But these appalling communications must be seen in perspective. Compared with those of twenty years ago, they are a tremendous improvement. Whereas then the nine hundred miles from Herat to Kabul could take ten days on the back of a lorry, it can now be done by car in a day and military road-building teams have hewn good roads out of mere narrow tracks in provinces like Paktya. In terms of immediate traffic there is perhaps no great need for very good provincial roads in a country where the bulk of transport is still by camel and donkey, horse and bullock cart, and where even great baulks of

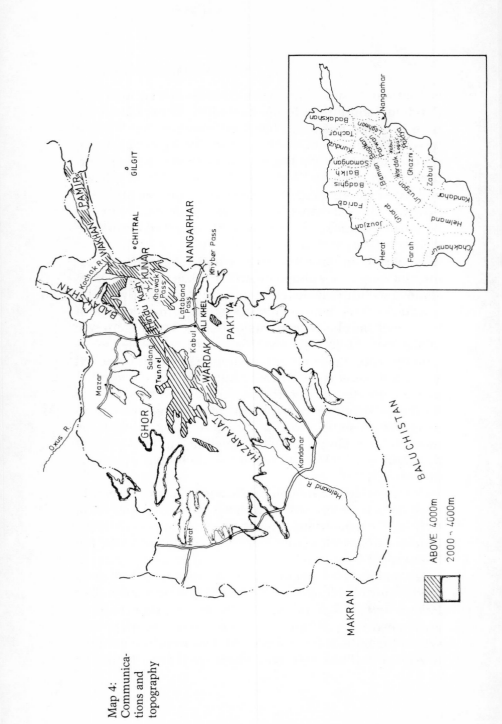

Map 4:
Communica-
tions and
topography

PAMIR

WAKHAN

GILGIT

BADAKHSHAN

Kochak R.

CHITRAL

Hindu Kush

KUNAR

NANGARHAR

Khawak Pass

Lataband Pass

Khyber Pass

Mazar

Salang Tunnel

Kabul

ALI KHEL

PAKTYA

Oxus R.

GHOR

WARDAK

HAZARAJAT

Kandahar

Helmand R.

Herat

BALUCHISTAN

MAKRAN

ABOVE 4000m

2000 ~ 4000m

Nangarhar

Badakshan

Takhar

Kunduz

Kabul

Laghman

Parwan

Kapisa

Bamian

Baghlan

Balkh

Samangan

Wardak

Ghazni

Logar

Uruzgan

Zabul

Badghis

Faryab

Ghorat

Jouzjan

Kandahar

Helmand

Chakhansur

Herat

Farah

cedar wood find their way to Pakistan, two or four at a
time, strapped to the sides of a camel. Thirty years ago
wheels of any kind, even on bicycles or potters wheels,
were unknown in the majority of Afghan villages. Yet in
terms of creating a sense of national unity and of promoting co-operation between the different provinces
and groups, the establishment of good communications
from province to province, as distinct from the direct
links with Kabul which are a permanent reminder of
provincial dependent status, is essential. The difficulties
and expense of such road-building programmes should
not be underestimated. These roads have to cross
deserts of shifting sand and stark black granite outcrops,
go over rivers whose spring floods can wash away a
solid stone bridge in a few minutes, and pierce mountains which climb to eighteen thousand feet. It may be
that railways – lacking in Afghanistan today – are a
good long-term investment and the Soviet aid programme provides for such a link across the Oxus and a
line from Iran via Herat and the Hajigak iron ore deposit
to Kabul. None of these alternatives is cheap and the
available bulk traffic is not sufficient to make a railway
economically viable for many years, though almost a
quarter of the expenditure in the proposed 1976/83
seven-year plan was earmarked for this project. Money
spent on fostering a sense of unity, however, is a sound
investment, even if it brings in its wake still greater
pressures from the provinces for a larger share of the national expenditure.

The present imbalance in favour of the Pathans, and
the official preoccupation with Pathan nationalism, can
only serve to alienate the minorities completely. This is
particularly true of the Uzbegs: a sophisticated and
capable people who provide the bulk of the country's
professional men and entrepreneurs. The amount of

private capital reinvested in the national economy is still, so far as it is measurable, pitifully small. The Uzbeg entrepreneur often feels no confidence in Afghanistan and its economy as a whole, feels he has no stake in the country and therefore often prefers to keep his surplus wealth in the local equivalent of a sock under the mattress. Such men have to be persuaded to invest in the economy by being given practical proof that they will have a reasonable say in its overall direction. Desperately short of capital resources, Afghanistan cannot afford to neglect internal private wealth. The development of industries associated with the discovery of natural gas at Shiberghan, right in the heart of the Uzbeg country near Mazar-i-Sharif, offers splendid opportunity for Uzbeg entrepeneurs to identify private with national interests. This, however, will be baulked unless there is a marked change of line in Kabul. If excessive emphasis is placed on ethnic affinities, and if it is legitimate in official circles for Pathan ambitions and interests to be projected southwards over the Pakistan border, then it can hardly be less legitimate for the Afghan Uzbegs to turn their eyes northwards across the Oxus to Russian Uzbekistan, where all their cultural affinities lie and whence, indeed, they derive their racial origins. One has only to witness their almost magical performance on horseback in their sport of *buzkashi* (which combines mounted mayhem with rugby football played with a beheaded goat) to realize that, in ethnic terms at least, their ties are with the horsemen of Soviet Central Asia.

In the early days of post-war economic penetration, the Russians were not slow to exploit this affinity by the extensive use of Russian Uzbegs in development projects in the relevant areas of Afghanistan; and, of course, those with radios are within reach of the ordinary domestic broadcasts of Soviet Uzbekistan. Clearly, any feeling of divided loyalties among such a powerful and capable minority would be fatal to hopes of Afghan unity; but it should be remembered that, while the sociologist, anthropologist and historian may look to the wider picture, the ordinary Uzbeg — for the present at least and despite the increasing influence of radio — is far more concerned with his immediate neighbours. But, as far as can be ascertained, resistance to the Russians in the Uzbeg areas is less than elsewhere.

The Hazaras, whose Mongoloid features and truculence of manner betray their descent from the hordes of Genghis Khan,* do not require the support of outside influences to strengthen their intransigence. Living in the central mountain area known as the Hazarajat (an extension of the Hindu Kush), they are almost literally inaccessible to all forms of central government or authority, from tax collection to police. The extent of their isolation can be judged by the discovery only a few years ago of a large, beautiful and historically important minaret near Jam; and the traveller trying to reach it may still enquire in vain at a village less than ten miles away. The isolation of the Hazaras is further aggravated by the fact that they alone of any major group of Afghans belong to the Shi'a sect of Islam, and are consequently despised by their Sunni fellow citizens. There are practically no employment possibilities in the Hazarajat; and this, since the area is largely barren, aggravates the discontent of the Hazaras. Official talk of a road (let alone a railway) linking Herat and Kabul through this area is still largely wishful thinking, but the discovery of large and very high-grade iron ore deposits at Hajigak near Bamian may in due course go some way to solve the employ-

---

*The exact nature of this descent is much disputed by ethnologists, but that the Hazaras are of Mongol origin is not in question.

ment problem and so bring the Hazaras within the conventional pattern of a modern state.

The largest of the principal minority groups, the Tajiks, are by tradition and inclination a peaceful people – poets, dreamers, intellectuals – who earn their living by farming in the regions round Kabul, Kandahar and Herat. They are proud of being Tajik in an unassertive way, and have a quiet and tactful courtesy towards strangers. Although they, like the Uzbegs, have links across the Oxus with their kindred in the Soviet Union, many of them emigrated to Afghanistan to escape from the persecution they suffered during the forced collectivization of the Soviet Union in the 1930s. If they have little love for the Pathans, and even founded a movement, Setem-i-Melli, against Pathan domination, they have even less for the Russians as their present fierce resistance indicates. Their attributes, like those of the other minorities, could be valuable ingredients in the emergence of the new Afghan nation for, if nations have characters, then there is no doubt that a balanced combination of the virtues, and even vices, of these four races could produce an impressive character indeed.

Across all these groupings, like a restless and repetitive air plucked on the metal-stringed *rebab*, runs the life of the nomads. Those dust clouds on the horizon, when you come closer, are seen to be living acres of sheep and goats, or a long line of camels piled high with tents and utensils with mother and child perched atop, for once enjoying a rarely experienced ease. The women, in their rich greens, veil themselves a little at the sight of strangers, although purdah is not their domestic practice since it inhibits their role as the family workers. The camels, gaily decked out with bridles of fine blue, white and red beads, are preceded at a jaunty trot by the dogs. Boys and men, each with a stout stick, ride their fine horses or walk around their flocks, since the dogs seem to have little herding skill. Soon they merge into the yellow haze again on their way to the high cool pastures of Badakshan. These are the nomads of the north. In the south, donkeys are perhaps more common than camels, rifles than knobbly sticks, women on foot than those riding. The colours are brighter and more varied, the column a little less orderly. North and south, the countryside is dotted with the nomads' flat tents which stand out like black blisters on the hot red flesh of the desert or merge into the background of dark hills; or perhaps they live in the round and carefully decorated felt huts of the more permanent settlements, into whose shadowy recesses the women disappear behind growling dogs at the first glimpse of a camera-bearing stranger.

It is not only on the frontiers with Pakistan that these nomads present problems. Since they are highly suspicious of any attempt to record their numbers or movements, for fear of making themselves more liable to government interference and control, such positive developments as education, medical services, agricultural improvement and parliamentary representation are rendered largely ineffectual in their case. They feel little loyalty to such an abstract concept as the state of Afghanistan or to its symbol of power, the Kabul-centred government. There is, in addition, a fierce rivalry of long standing between the Ghilzai and the ruling Durrani tribes.

The fissiparous tendencies in Afghanistan became dramatically evident during the student riots of October 1965. A very shrewd American observer told me that the students naively believed that the armed police, mostly Uzbegs and Hazaras, would not be brutal to them or fire on demonstrating fellow countrymen, albeit Pathans. In fact, my informant told me, the police – simple country lads for the most part – revelled in the chance to 'have a go' at the city-slickers from the Pathan capital of Kabul.

The problem facing Afghan governments is an intractable one, for it is precisely those Pathan characteristics making for efficient exercise of authority that also make unity among the different races difficult to obtain. There can be little amity and sense of common purpose when one race feels itself innately superior to the others, whom it considers as irremediably second-class citizens. However, this attitude probably holds good only in a primitive agricultural and tribal society. The modernization, industrialization and urbanization of Afghanistan may eventually undermine this almost colonial relationship.

The great contrasts between wealth and poverty common to most underdeveloped countries are scarcely evident in Afghanistan. This is because even the middle and upper classes, or the majority of individuals among them, are relatively poor and because outlets for conspicuous consumption are few. Buildings, carpets, flocks and land and, in the north, the superb *buzkashi* horses on which a man will gladly spend a small fortune – these are almost the only investments for accumulated wealth. There is still virtually no private industrial and commercial large-scale investment, and the commodities on which, in a consumer economy, the rich spend their wealth are still not easy to obtain in Afghanistan, outside Kabul and one or two other urban centres, due to lack of foreign exchange. Indeed, it is quite likely that the nomad families with the largest herds are among the richest people in Afghanistan, although their wealth cannot really be converted to measurable terms.

Yet, if evidence of the heights of wealth is scarce, it is

equally rare in Afghanistan to come across any stark display of the depths of poverty which are so harrowing in more densely populated, if richer, underdeveloped countries. The children, boys and girls, are generally well cared for and fed, and are almost extravagantly well clothed. The signs of disease are plentiful, but the emaciated limbs and swollen stomachs of severe malnutrition are rare. There is some begging, but not the persistent buzzing swarm of importunate human flies common to other Eastern countries. It is not easy, either, to tell rich from poor, or at least from relatively poor, by outward appearances. Their style of dress and diet is much the same, and their houses, although different in scale, are usually similar in external appearance and design. In Kabul, it is true, distinctions are beginning to emerge, but only because the capital is ceasing in many ways to be typically Afghan and is acquiring some of the depressingly identical cosmopolitan features of all capital cities.

More objective assessment of poverty levels is hard to make in a land where fiction is preferred to figures.* A World Bank team estimated in 1977 that 85 dollars a year was needed to cover basic necessities and that be-

---

*Too much reliance should not be placed on Afghan statistics. Public enterprises seldom keep meaningful accounts and governments tend to substitute forecasts and wishful thinking for actual measurement of past accomplishment. For more recent figures I have drawn chiefly on an excellent report by the World Bank written in 1977 and published in March 1978 and on Maxwell Fry's book *The Afghan Economy* (published by E.J. Brill, Leyden, 1974). It seemed pointless to include figures after the Taraki coup in 1978 in almost all instances, as the disruption of the economy and the even more than usually strident demands of propaganda made them meaningless in any long term context. Thus when the word 'now' is stated or implied in the text, it is taken to mean 1977/78.

tween 20% and 40% of the population fell below this poverty line. Average income per head was 120 dollars, though double that in Kabul, and GNP per head 160 dollars. The average Afghan spends two-thirds of his income on food and owing to the severity of the climate 10% on fuel and a further 10% on clothing. In the rural areas,. however, his house, made of mud and straw brick, will account for only just over 1% of his income.

When every Pathan is a prince in his own eyes, and men of other races are strong in personal pride, it is not easy for the casual observer to detect local equivalents of those class differences that abound, with all their social minutiae, in western societies. Evidence of a racial hierarchy we have already noted; the hierarchies within each community are much harder to detect. Where these exist, they tend to be expressed in the form of offical positions in the administrative and government structure, for government activity embraces a far wider spectrum of activity than it does in Britain, for example. These positions in turn frequently depend on nepotism (it was thus pleasantly surprising in the 60s to meet the Finance Minister's nephew doctoring in one of the remotest provinces) and on the extremely complex patterns of family relationships and rivalries, of which the blood feud has only been the most dramatic expression.

The art of family power politics depends largely upon the ability to marry off the women of the family in such a judicious way as to keep its wealth intact, and for the men to marry in such a way as to increase the family fortunes. The ramifications that these marriages have led to over the generations are almost impossible for the stranger to follow. In effect, however, for the 'class' distinctions of western society one can substitute the word 'family', if one is seeking out special divisions and barriers. The privileged members of Afghan society come from no more than a dozen or so families, but 'family' has to be interpreted very widely to include degrees of cousinship which would scarcely be traceable in western society. Even so, it can fairly be said that Afghanistan does not suffer from those two divisive plagues of western society: class antagonism and wealth snobbery.

The most strikingly obvious divisions in Afghanistan, are between the sexes. 'Eve span and Adam dozed' might be the proverb here, for while the men sit around chatting in the *chai khanas,* the women do much of the day-to-day work, not only of the house, but of the field. This inequality is enshrined in the system of purdah: a conception which, incidentally, is quite alien to the pristine tenets of Islam. Purdah is not merely the wearing of the all-enveloping *chadhuri;** this sartorial isolation only symbolizes the whole position of women in Afghan society as inferior beings set apart, automative chattels. The setting apart of women extends to every aspect of life: their rooms, their meals, their upbringing. Even in their love life their status as amatory partner is usually re-

---

*The all-enveloping *chadhuri* makes a woman look like a walking beachtent or a child playing ghosts with the bed linen. Such, at least, it appears to one male eye. For a technical description, I am grateful to be able to quote that of the wife of a former Minister of the Interior. 'It is a garment that has a cap which is usually very intricately embroidered, and from this falls yards and yards of material minutely pleated, like umbrella pleating in a skirt. Then in front of the face there is an embroidered section like a net, the embroidery so worked that the holes are large enough for the wearer to see through. Then there is a heavily embroidered piece falling down to the waist. The whole garment has such a wide skirt that it can be pulled around the wearer so that no part of her can be seen except her feet as she walks.' One might think the garment, though cumbrous, is apt to keep out dust and heat: I am told this is not so. (The garment is also called *burqa*.)

garded as inferior to that of the male, whose universal jealousy can often be so extreme as to make poor Othello seem like a complacent cuckold. A man's love affair is as likely to involve another man or boy as a woman. Many of the poems of the great Pushtu poet, Khushal Khan, are unequivocally and unashamedly written to youths.

Purdah is basically an urban phenomenon, less stringently practised and enforced in the villages, and by the nomads scarcely at all. Its extension and retention are at least partly the fault of the women themselves, in the view of one shrewd lady (a foreigner married for many years to a very prominent Afghan). The *chadhuri* was seen as a social status symbol and the poorer women, particularly peasants moving into towns, would obtain one as soon as they possibly could in order to imitate their city sisters whom they regarded as their social superiors. Certainly, the *chadhuri* is a great equalizer among women since it gives the ugly ones a chance. But differences in the material and workmanship, and the air of wearing it by one passing purdahed woman as against another, are nevertheless apparent.

Afghan women have been officially quite free to dispense with the *chadhuri* since Daoud's 1959 pronouncement to this effect began the tactfully gradual introduction of female emanicipation. Soon the brave among the more prominent women were showing the way and others followed suit. Yet, even today, in towns other than Kabul you will see the majority of the women still wearing the *chadhuri*. If you travel in the provinces, you will find very few women who will go without it in public. In the bigger provincial towns women, even foreign visitors, will sometimes attract contemptuous comment from the male bystanders if they are unveiled. Remonstrance that the unveiled one is only following royal precept leaves them unmoved, for the Afghan man is no fool and sees the immediate implications of the disappearance of purdah for his own easy way of life. Unfortunately, few of them have yet seen that, in the long run, purdah can only hamper the growth of their prosperity.

Purdah in Afghanistan is based on the concept of a woman as a man's property. The governor of one district (Chahardarra in the province of Kunduz) explained to me with some pride in 1966, the way in which the region's beautiful handwoven carpets were made; how five or six women might work together for four or five months to make a patterned carpet, nine feet by six feet, for which they would get 4,600 afghanis*, and how a man would pay a very good bride-price for a girl who was an accomplished carpet weaver. When I asked him who got the money for the carpets, he looked at me in astonishment and replied: 'Why the man of course, the woman belongs to the man.' Some of the nomads even tatoo on their women the same mark they put on their sheep! It is this attitude which is the chief obstacle facing the champions of women's emancipation in Afghanistan.

Those who dislike the idea of feminine equality, but do not wish to oppose it outright, adopt many subtle arguments. They ask why there is any need for emancipation when Afghan women already wield so much power within the family. After all, it is the women who arrange the all important marriages on which the family fortunes may depend, and it is often the oldest woman in the family to whom all its members hand over their earnings and wealth for her to manage and augment. She

---

*The carpet would sell at two to five times this price in the bazaar at Kabul, and for ten to twenty times as much by the time it reached a European or American drawing room.

it is who in many cases holds the family purse strings. But these are subtle sophistries, for such power is exercised only on sufferance or by strength of will, not as a recognized right. In fact, it is this very family structure which helps to perpetuate the inferior role of women. The value of a marriage arrangement often depends on the fact that a woman has no property rights in marriage, and that property, therefore, reverts to the male side of the family when a woman dies — contrary as this is to the Shari'at.

Under the old customs, it was virtually impossible for a girl to refuse to marry the man of her parents' choice, for the marriage was seen as an important property transaction, one not to be thwarted by mere personal whim. Moreover, the parents could invoke the law to support them in any conflict with an erring daughter who decided she did not fancy her betrothed. Today, however, although most marriages are still arranged — and are not necessarily the less happy for that — the girl's wishes are normally consulted and no penalty is exacted for refusing to comply with the parental will. More matches are made, too, on the initiative of the man and woman themselves, for love. The shy pride of a doctor or a teacher who tells you he married for love is something new on the Afghan scene.

There are two major weapons in the Afghan emancipator's armoury: education and economic opportunity. Through the first they can encourage the women to rebel against their inferior status, through the second to rebel successfully. It is significant that practically all the leading women in Afghan public life in the democratic period had been teachers of one kind or another, and were concentrating their efforts on creating wider educational opportunities for girls. These, at present, are very limited.

Women have just begun to break through into the professions. There are a few women doctors, and one or two women engineers; women nurses, health visitors and malaria control officers are coming forward in increasing numbers – in 1977 there were about two hundred. But here the problem is always the same: to get them to go out into the provinces and the villages where their influence is most desperately needed. Husbands and brothers still generally refuse to let a woman involved in medical work stay away from home overnight. (Treatment at second hand, where the doctor is a man and the patient is a woman, is still practised in many areas; the husband or father relays questions from the doctor, symptoms from the patient and treatment back from the doctor, without doctor and patient ever meeting face to face.) Life is not easy for the woman who goes to the provinces and the counter-attractions of Kabul are very strong: not only the amenities and services, and the better health of her children, but the fact that in Kabul she is one of many women tasting freedom. In the provinces she will often be a lonely and conspicuous pioneer. If she wants to further her education, her chance of doing so in the provinces is very small. The provision of such opportunity is thus a critical point in changing women's traditional role in Afghanistan.

Yet education, without economic opportunity, is not enough. If she is to have the courage to assert her right to live her own life, a woman must be able to feel confident that she can defy her family and social pressures and taboos, and yet still make her own living independently. She will also want to appear attractive out of purdah, to have good clothes, shoes and make-up now that her form and features no longer lurk behind the *chadhuri* – and this costs money. In law, an Afghan woman is entitled to equal pay for equal work; in practice (as is not unknown in more progressive societies), she does not get it.

In the first place, there is very little work that a woman can take up outside the 'ministering' activities of medicine and education – air hostessing must probably be counted as 'ministrative' too. The most important and rapidly expanding new field is secretarial work, for which, with the modernization of Afghan industry and commerce, there is an increasing and unsatisfied demand. There are also a few women employed in manufacturing – as opposed to cottage – industry, particularly in the Spinzar Company's pottery works in Kunduz, and in some textile processes. But here, also, the inequalities are evident. Woman pottery workers with four years' experience of doing the delicate trimming operations on the unfired teapots and jugs, for which most men's hands are too clumsy, earn only about two-thirds of the pay of men doing similar and, if anything, slightly less delicate work further down the production line, although in theory they should receive equal pay for equal work. Criticism of the Spinzar Company for this disparity has to be tempered by the recognition that it was a real pioneer in employing women at all. Credit must be given, too, for its ingenuity in starting this employment in a field where even the most censorious anti-feminist has to concede that women are guiltless of the crime of rivalling men, because men, in fact, are incapable of doing the work. In the country where the sudden and sweeping reforms introduced by Amanullah came to such a disastrous end, it seems as if a gradual, pragmatic approach may be successful.

The full rigours of purdah are normally imposed at the onset of puberty, a little before the age of twelve, when the great majority of Afghan girls leave school. The provision of further education and training institutions to bridge the gap between the school-leaving age and taking up relatively independent employment at, say, fifteen or sixteen is of critical importance, for it will enable

(Top) The capital of the old Raj may be very distant but its influence still pervades much of the frontier. (Bottom) Hazards such as this were the commonplace of travellers in Afghanistan twenty years ago and still have to be faced whenever the main road route is abandoned.

In Paktya, as in so many parts of Afghanistan, a rifle is as natural a part of walking-out attire as a stick.

A relic of earlier times, this gun was deployed by a young English lieutenant to hold off a Russian inspired Persian attack on Herat.

The wooded hills of Paktya provide not only timber for smuggling into Pakistan but ideal guerrilla cover.

the girls to evade the start of purdah. Once this has been accomplished, it is much easier for them to maintain their emancipated condition. The spearhead of the emancipation campaign is the girl in this category, supported by girls from enlightened families in which purdah is abolished. Manpower shortage in the unskilled categories is certainly not an Afghan problem at present. It remains true, however, that an underdeveloped country has little chance of making substantial progress unless it has freed the energies of its women so that these can be applied to national objectives.

A number of remarkable individual women, some of them foreigners, have campaigned for women's rights in Afghanistan over the past thirty years. Its most prominent leaders in the mid-60's were the four women deputies elected to the Wolesi Jirgah, the lower house of the Shura (parliament), in the elections of October 1965. In these, women were both allowed to vote and to stand, although not many took advantage of their rights to do either. One of the women deputies for an area just outside Kandahar was certain that, in fact, not a single woman had supported her. (Her election was due to the last-minute withdrawal in her favour of the two male opponents.) The others were opposed by men; remarkable as it must seem, they were elected by a predominantly male electorate. These four women deputies – Mrs Mahsuma Wardaki, Mrs Rokyan Abu Bakr, Dr Anahita Ratebzad and Mrs Adija – made a considerable impact in parliament, showing themselves the equals of the best men deputies. Their influence was principally exerted in the areas of special interest to them, such as education and women's welfare, but it was not confined to these.

Putting their views on the role of women in Afghanistan to me at that time, Mrs Wardaki and Mrs Abu Bakr argued most cogently that the inferior position of

women in Afghan society offends against both the constitution of the state and the religion of Islam. The constitution demands that laws and government should
conform to the laws of Islam. The laws of Islam, the
emancipators argue, protect the rights and status of
women; hence, to the extent that the exploitation and
domination of women is permitted in it, Afghanistan is
an 'ungodly' state in which the tenets of Islam and their
constitutional validity are being questioned.

It would need an expert in Islamic lore to appraise this
'liberal Muslim' argument properly. It is certainly
arguable that there is less scriptural justification for the
inferior status of women in the Koran than in the New
Testament, where Saint Paul makes it very plain that
wives should be in subjection to their husbands. Particularly striking is the way in which the Koran
specifically mentions 'men' and 'women' separately
rather than collectively in setting out such matters as
rights to property and access to Paradise (e.g. *Surat al-
Tauba*, v. 71 *et seq*). On the other hand, there is the
positive statement (*Surat al-Nisa*, v. 23) that 'the men are
set over the women' – although theologians have ex-
pended much energy in arguing just what 'set over'
means in this context. The sympathetic Westerner may
well feel that, in the Afghan situation, these niceties of
theological debate are less important than the fact that
the women deputies at least made a pre-emptive bid
against those conservatives in the Shura who opposed
emancipatory reforms on the grounds that they were
contrary to Islam.

The argument of the emancipators may have been
subtle but it did not carry much weight with the
mullahs, the religious leaders, for these have come to
epitomize in the name of Islam, the conservative opposition to female emancipation, and played no small role in

seeing that no female deputies were elected to the 1969 Wolesi Jirgah.

'When these reforms come in, Islam will go out', declared one angry mullah and was promptly clapped in prison by Amir Amanullah, whose rash attempts to make Afghanistan a modern state overnight, with equality between the sexes, secularized education and democratic institutions, had provoked this declaration. But the mullah had the last laugh, for the rising inspired by his fellow mullahs succeeded in putting the clock back again, and in due course Amanullah lost his throne.

Until the overthrow of Daoud in 1978 these reforms were being reintroduced, more subtly, more effectively, and in a more welcoming climate of public opinion. The more overt commitment to emancipation of subsequent despised Marxist régimes may well have set back, rather than advanced, women's cause. Is it still right to assume with the mullah that Islam and the progressive social development of a modern state are incompatible? If it is, what will the outcome of the conflict be? Now, as in the past, the role of the mullahs is critical. They, after all, are the interpreters of the Koran and of the Islamic faith to a simple people. If they claim that the woman's role is properly an inferior one, will it make any difference for militant females and liberal scholars to declare that such a conception is contrary to the true doctrines of Islam?

Islam has no ordained priesthood but rather a pastorate of knowledge – though it is permissible to refrain from adding 'and of wisdom', for often there is but little of it. The original thinker, particularly in Sunni Afghanistan, is looked on as a dangerous man, for the whole pattern of religious learning is based on a process of repetitive ingestion and regurgitation, generation after generation, of the same arguments and doctrines with no attempt to adapt them to changing circumstances. Such a dogmatic process of instruction, exercised on those generally drawn from the lower and peasant class, tends to lead to bigotry and narrowmindedness, in things temporal as well as spiritual. Anything which falls outside the compass of recorded knowledge and has no precise precedent is, for the mullahs, either insignificant or inimical. It would be wrong to suggest that there are no good and wise men among the mullahs, but the significant point is that training and circumstances reinforce the limitations of the mediocre who form the great majority.

Most are illiterate farmers and only part-time pastors, indeed, they sometimes seem rather to be *Shamans*, dealing in white magic, than religious leaders. The traffic in bogus and magical relics at many local shrines is quite as extensive as was that in Chaucer's 'Pigges bones' and provides one of the many sources of material comforts and secular power which the mullahs now fight so fanatically to protect. Among other privileges in this category they are particularly jealous of the system by which, like the mediaeval monasteries in Britain, they are able to own land under the guise of religious, tax-exempt endowments (*wafqs*).

There are an awesome multitude of detailed rules for the conduct of private and civil life which have to be learned by the mullah, and such is the number and complexity of these rules that the ordinary citizen who wishes to conduct his life in accordance with Koran and Sunna has no option but to seek the mullah's guidance. Indeed, the Muslim's word for priesthood, in the Sunni persuasion at least, is *ulama* or 'knowers'. The mullah has often been the only focus of law and learning in many a village and small town. Since the law is based on the Koran, the mullah lays claim not only to the authority which comes with the power of moral and spiritual judgement and leadership, but also to the authority derived from his role as an interpreter, however indirect, of the law governing the daily lives of the villagers. Moreover, the *madrasah* system of education has for long given the mullah a position of authority vis-à-vis the local people from childhood onward; in this system, the mosque and the school are virtually synonymous, and the method of learning applied is a miniature reflection of the pattern of the mullah's own education. Until very recently, this sterile form of rote learning was the only one available.

To be fair, an oral tradition of learning is inevitable in a country where so few can read and write. Illiteracy, in that sense, has largely resisted various attempts by central government to reduce it. Bureaucracy as a main weapon of control in the twentieth-century corporate state requires the citizen to be able to read his orders and fill in his forms; oral traditions confine obedience to earshot and the village mullah has, radio apart, the loudest voice. It is difficult to be precise about such figures, but probably only one-eighth of the population can read and write. One man in five, but less than one woman in twenty-five may be able to do both, and of those over forty virtually none. Four-fifths of the population have never been to school and that figure for women is over 90%. Of course, things are better the further down the age scale you go, and half the Afghan population is under fifteen. Something like half the ten-year-old boys have attended school and though only 5% to 10% of the girls in the same age group have been to school, this is a vast improvement on the education of girls as little as fifteen years ago. In 1975 there were some 700,000 children in the 3,300 primary and village schools. This represents about one-third of the age group. Or to put it another way, about half a million boys aged seven to twelve and a million girls are receiving *no* formal education. 170,000 are receiving secondary education and 11,000 higher education, though it must be recognized that this latter category ranges in standard from about fifth form level at a British secondary school to genuine university work.

The government, through the Ministry of Education, chooses who shall have the higher education places, it decides what course of study a student shall pursue and exacts in payment almost a lifetime of compulsory government service from graduates who may not be free to strike out on their own until their fifties.

But social and geographical mobility also plays its part in the power of local influences when set against central government wishes. Over four-fifths of the population lives in the countryside and the same proportion lives, and has only lived, within a few miles of where they were born. Three-quarters of all Afghans live in the very village or town in which they were born. Influences established in youth thus remain paramount throughout adulthood and the whole pattern of family life − 99% of all Afghans marry − is designed to keep them so. The centre of that local authority is the village mullah.

Up to the first generation of this century, when the authority of the mullahs was at its most formidable, they had it in their power to rouse the people to war with their cries of 'Islam in danger', and often did so. Religion was very much an ingredient in the perennial border clashes with British India, the Afghan War of Independence of 1919 and the revolutionary overthrow of the would-be reforming Amanullah in 1929. Even twenty years ago, the authority of the mullah and respect for him were virtually unquestioned in Afghanistan. He could jab a clear space for himself with his umbrella in the back of a dangerously overcrowded lorry without protest, and the foreigner who forcefully objected was in danger of being thrown off by the other passengers as an impudent *feringi*. The mullahs are still the mainstay of the conservative opposition to reform, indeed to change of any kind. Often ignorant and bigoted men, they are at least shrewd enough to realize that reform can only mean the end of their almost exclusive authority and a decline in their status. The sequence of increasingly secular, socialist and foreign dominated governments that followed Daoud's coup in 1973, has given them great opportunities to recover lost ground in the name of Islam, culminating once more in the cry of 'Islam in danger' and the call to *Jihad* against the invading Russians. Whether they could hold the ground regained under a reformist, *independent* Afghan government is another matter.

A decline in the influence of the mullahs had been taking place over the past two decades, so much so that they were no longer in a position to veto all progess, provided changes were made gradually and tactfully. The main reason for this decline in influence was the growth of alternative sources for the authority and educational opportunity of which the mullahs once had a monopoly. Education, albeit still in very short supply, is available through state schools, where the tenets of Islam are certainly still taught, but learning them by heart is no longer the only mode of instruction. As the economic and political structure of the country becomes more complex, so the tentacles of administrative, secular authority reach out further and further into the rural areas. The law is becoming more a matter of police and lawyers, legislation, courts and judges; although still based on the Koran, it has an increasingly secular flavour, in which nice legal arguments about evidence have replaced precedented but inflexible interpretations of the Divine Will.

The gradual decline in the influence of the mullahs does not necessarily imply any decline in the importance of the Islamic faith in Afghanistan. The seemingly inevitable divorce between religion and everyday life which accompanies the urbanization and industrialization of a simple rural society is only occasionally in evidence in Afghanistan. Belief in Islam and the practice of its rituals is still the almost invariable rule throughout the country. Admittedly, one notices the slight secularization – if that is the right word – of some members of the upper and middle class. A bottle of Scotch will appear on the table and be drunk as willingly by the influential Muslim host as by his guest. A scientist will admit to scepticism; a government official will regret that he feels Islam an anachronism in the context of social progress. (This latter argument will sometimes meet with the riposte that a return to the original purity of Islamic doctrine would, in fact, be conducive to progress – as, for instance, in the case of the status of women.)

But these few, sceptics and reformers alike, are the exceptions. The great mass of the people accept and believe in Islam in exactly the form that their fathers have done for many generations, ever since their conversion at sword-point in the tenth century AD. There is no mistaking the way in which Islam has become a deep-rooted part of Afghan life. 'Please excuse me while I say my prayers', says your host, gesturing for you to continue drinking your tea while he turns away into a corner, thus fitting his religion naturally into his daily life. Or perhaps it is the touching simplicity of the nomad who walks a little apart from his flock and kneels on his prayer mat, his brown clothes and black *pugri* standing out starkly against the evening skyline, to say the prescribed prayers; or that same mullah who so uncharitably wielded his umbrella and who now climbs down from the lorry in some isolated clump of huts and under the single tree leads the villagers in prayer by lantern light.

For the Afghans, the observances of Islam are an integral part of life's daily routine. Yet the observances are perhaps more important to them than the faith. Sometimes you cannot help feeling that the gesture of the hands spread behind the ears is indicative of nothing so much as the worshipper's own deafness to the strident cries of a new world. The mosques, of which there are some fifteen thousand in Afghanistan, are coolly beautiful. The pale blue and dark green glazed tiles, the simple curved architecture, the pleasantly laid-out gardens, have all the dark unhurried calm which befits a place of worship. Yet how far is it the quiet of decay rather than of tranquillity? I could not help feeling in Afghanistan (and must admit to knowing too little of Islam for anything but impressions) that the centuries-old faith had lost the capacity for change and would be left behind in the Middle Ages when every other aspect of national life had finally made its painful way into the twentieth century.

Other faiths are tolerated in Afghanistan, but this is largely a gesture to foreigners. Of the great faiths that were once universal in Afghanistan (like Buddhism) or had their origins there (like Zoroastrianism), there is scarcely a trace of either relic or practice today. Islam is perhaps a little more isolated in Afghanistan than it is in other Muslim countries. There is little truck with the Shi'a doctrines paramount in neighbouring Persia; indeed, these are looked on by the strictly orthodox Sunni Afghans as effete and corrupt. This attitude is an additional factor in the antagonism between the Pathans and the Hazaras, the latter being Afghanistan's only major Shi'a group.* Nor does Afghanistan seem to make much of the brotherhood of Islamic nations, perhaps because its major source of international disagreement is with one of them. This may account for the apparent Arab reluctance to fund the resistance to the Soviet invasion – even Saudi Arabia's May 1980 gift of twenty-five million dollars was mainly for refugee relief.

Of that trio of tolerances so frequently invoked in human rights' charters – 'without discrimination in regard to race, sex or creed' – the first two, in Afghanistan, may be divisive factors; but the third, the religion of Islam, is very definitely a unifying factor. It is the major cultural and spiritual common denominator of ethnic groups that otherwise have little in common. But, although it is a unifying factor which enables the government to relate laws and administration to an acceptable premise, understood, however dimly, by all the people, it is not, as some would wish, necessarily a barrier to the communism of its giant neighbour. The argument is that being so strongly theistic, a Muslim country provides no vacuum for the materialistic doctrines of communism to occupy. Yet, in many respects, Islam itself is a materialistic faith, and the dogmatic nature of its belief may be in keeping with the dogmatic approach of communism. Perhaps Islam, in its rigid and materialistic forms, is sufficiently similar to certain features in communism for the one to open the way for the other. There is, however, a major factor which has hampered the spread of communism in Afghanistan: the

---

*There are also some very small Pathan tribal groups that are Shi'a, but most of these live on the Pakistan side of the border, and some scattered groups who adhere to the Ismaili faith.

fact that there Islam is the faith of a fiercely independent group of individualists. It is this individualism that provides the antithesis to communism rather than religious doctrine as such.

There are two other elements it is necessary to consider in order to appreciate the social background to current events in Afghanistan. The *Pushtunwali,* or code of honour, which dictates the conduct of life quite as much as religion or government in the Pathan areas of Afghanistan and the process by which administration, and particularly the law, has been centralized during the twentieth century.

The Pathan code of honour has its minor variations from tribe to tribe but its central core revolves round the twin concepts of honour and what I term aptness in the aesthetic sense. The ideal man is the warrior poet, the man bold in battle, eloquent in counsel and moving in love – whether of male or female. Woman scarcely features except in so far as she is either the recipient of the benefits of the *Pushtunwali,* or bound, through her menfolk, by its obligations. But she is also, to some extent, the guardian of its standards, usually in her role as mother, paying blood money or denouncing the cowardice of a son.

The element the traveller in Afghanistan most often encounters is that of hospitality, an element which in my experience has rubbed off equally on the non-Pathans. The code obliges a man to be hospitable whenever the occasion offers and I have often been lodged and entertained by a villager who would not think twice before killing his last chicken for your supper and whom it is very hard to recompense in any way without offending. The most important extension of this part of the code is the obligation to protect, with your life if necessary, the person and property of your guest and if he specifically takes refuge with you, to take up his cause as well.

The second major element of the code, perhaps rather the first if more rare than sometimes supposed, is the obligation to avenge the spilling of blood. This is not just a matter of a death for a death, but in lesser degree of an eye for an eye – or a tooth for a tooth! Such revenge quarrels can continue for many generations and to some extent serve as both a safety valve and a proving ground for manhood in a society where a boy has a gun put into his hand not so very long after he can walk. Surprisingly few are actually killed in the fairly frequent inter-village or inter-tribal conflicts, which if not triggered by a feud usually centre on the right to water or land. In the context of the blood feud the Russians are building up a debt which will not easily be redeemed.

A third element is, strange as it may seem, the concept of mercy. One does not kill women (adultresses excepted) or small children, a poet or a Hindu, a priest or a man who has taken sanctuary in a mosque. Except where a blood feud is involved – and here only blood money will clear the debt – mercy is granted at the intercession of a woman or a priest and in battle even of the opponent himself when he begs for it. This last point may seem to contrast oddly with the bloodthirsty 'no prisoners' talk of guerrilla leaders (fervently believed by the ordinary Russian soldier) and the sadistic tortures and inhumane killings for which the Pathan was and still is renowned. Perhaps the hardest thing about the *Pushtunwali* is to know to whom it extends, for that so often seems to depend on the whim of the man with the dagger in his hand.

No central government can clearly tolerate for long the quasi-anarchical state implicit in the *Pushtunwali,* so the struggle for control between the central authority

and the tribes is a very old one. In this century the centre has gradually, with many setbacks, begun to assert
its supremacy. This process began in the late nineteenth
century with the remarkable Abdur Rahman, who early
in his reign declared that his unifying aim 'was to impose
law and order on all those hundreds of petty chiefs,
plunderers, robbers and cut throats. This necessitates
breaking down the feudal and tribal systems and
substituting one grand entity under one law and one
rule.'[1]

To this end he created a regular national army, police
and civil service who were in a way the embryo of the
first Afghan nationalists. Their first major test came in
1891, when the ever recalcitrant Hazaras continued to
ignore central legal and fiscal authority and resisted
those sent to enforce it. Abdur Rahman sent in his troops
and at first the Hazaras did not resist them. However,
when the Pathan troops got out of hand and seized property and women, a fierce and bloody rebellion broke out
which was not finally put down until 1893. The victors
turned over much Hazara pasture to the Kuchi nomads
and sold many of them into slavery. More significantly,
in the long term they imposed the rule of law on the
basis of their own particular Sunni interpretation, which
was an anathema to the Shi'a Hazaras, and broke the influence of the local leaders. That pattern has continued
ever since, though even today, throughout Afghanistan,
the local Khans still provide some protection for the villagers against the not infrequent depredations of op-
pressive or corrupt government or central officials.

The counterpoint of local custom and central fiat,
variety and consistency, wove its varied balance at least
up until the closing stages of Daoud's second period of
rule.

A good illustration of the practical realities of this

system was the story told me in 1966 by Muhammad Hussein Massa, Governor of Balkh, about 'the tooth that did not fit'. Sitting on his verandah in Mazar-i-Sharif one day, he was suddenly confronted by an agitated citizen who claimed that he had been grievously assaulted and that the Governor must compel his assailant to recompense him financially. The Governor calmed him and bade him sit down and tell his story. This the complainant did with a wealth of graphic detail, his tale reaching its climax with the dramatic production of the tooth which the assailant was supposed to have struck from the victim's mouth.

'Indeed a monstrous blow,' said the Governor, examining the tooth with great solicitude. 'Tell me, from which part of your mouth was it struck? Please show me the wound.'

Taken aback, the complainant thought hastily and then pointed to a gap in his teeth.

'But see,' said the Governor, 'the tooth does not fit. Now stop wasting my time and yours and go and devote your energy and ingenuity to more useful ends.'

In a still simple society of isolated communities, much depends on the ability, percipience and sympathy of the man on the spot. Afghanistan was blessed during the 60s with a number of capable administrators throughout the provinces, but they were far too few for the ever growing tasks put on them by increasingly dirigiste governments in the 1970s. Indeed, few things impressed me more at that time than the calibre of the top officials I met, at my own request, throughout the country. The Governor of Balkh, it is true, had been the very successful Minister of Mines and Power in the Yusuf administration, in which post he had been largely responsible for the launching of the natural gas industry; but other governors, from Kunduz to Paktya, proved almost without exception to be as able. The governorship of a province was not strictly a civil service type of post; for instance, there was no ban on a governor's continuing to participate in political life while he held office.

The provincial governor, almost invariably very short staffed, had a two-pronged administrative machine. The first prong was that of his direct decison-making. The majority of decisions in the practical fields of agriculture, industry, irrigation, mining and so on were reached in conjunction with the representatives on the spot of the appropriate ministries and not often referred back to Kabul. In this relationship, the governor usually took the initiative. Both governor and departmental representative were working within the limitation of the budgetry allocation under the particular departmental heading for their province. There is no local revenue, although the national revenue through taxation is gathered as a provincial responsibility. The various ministries were given their share of the national budget and then allocated this to different projects in the provinces. Hitherto, the initiative for these projects has been largely ministerial, although the detail of their application has been worked out at local level. But the provinces themselves were latterly encouraged to propose schemes of development, though with the revenue of the provincial municipalities accounting for no more than 1% of total state revenues, their scope for *independent* initiative was neglible. The other prong of the provincial governor's administrative machine was provided through a series of district governors in charge of various sections of his province. They worked to his orders and had their own small staff.

The system demanded that both the greater and the lesser governor be accessible to the people of the province or district. It was a common sight, in the Pathan areas in particular, to find the local district governor being buttonholed in the street (literally, for he was probably the only one wearing European dress) by some loquacious citizen and urged to do or prevent something. Not that the Pathans are spineless beseechers of authority when some grievance exercises their concern; far from it. As one district governor pointed out to me, such is the initiative of the Pathan and his extraordinary capacity for voluntary corporate activity that, as often as not, the job has been done by the time the governor has even heard that it needs to be done.

The dialogue between governor and governed was formalized through elected Provincial Councils. But in most provinces the real power and initiative still lay mainly in the hands of the governor. The remarkable thing was that the governors were quite willing to be guided in many things by public opinion in the various forms in which it was expressed to them, until in the late 70s they found themselves increasingly at odds with local leaders and more responsible for the maintenance of law and order than for the promotion of prosperity.

During the 'democratic' period power was further centralized by diminishing local autonomy on matters of policing and local administration of the law, though these remained primarily the provincial governor's responsiblity. He could also call in the military if he thought its help necessary to maintain public order, but he had no direct authority over the military in his province. The picture in this respect was a little ambiguous in those Pathan tribal areas where the administration was military and the governor a senior military officer, although at district level the military administrator acted to all intents and purposes as a civilian. Further confusion arose with the creation of a police investigation department directly responsible to the Attorney-

General's office and not the provincial governor's. A certain amount of antagonism developed as a result of this division. The local police, at that time generally unarmed, felt that, despite their particular knowledge of the area, they were being relegated to an inferior peace-keeping position. The Attorney-General's department, by contrast, viewed its activities as an independent assurance of the objective investigation of a charge or a crime. The representative of the Attorney-General acted rather in the capacity of the French 'Juge d'instruction', as both prosecutor and judge in examinations of first instance, but it was always open to the accused to appeal from his decisions to a higher court. Similarly, a tribesman could technically appeal to his district governor against a fine enforced by the local Jirgah, but he got short shrift from governor and fellow citizens alike in most cases. A determined man could take the matter still further by appeal to the provincial governor or to the courts.

The major legal problem in Afghanistan has been to ensure the application of a 'common' law to all parts of the country: a problem arising, not so much from abuse – although in the past the Afghan judiciary has certainly been open to corruption – as from tribal customs. In Pathan districts, the law has been a combination of custom and personal justice assessed by the local Jirgah, or Council. It worked very often on the basis of 'everybody knows that so-and-so did such-and-such' rather than on careful accumulations of evidence. It contained a highly compensatory rather than a purely punitive element, and was much concerned with personal honour. The story of the old woman who, when her great-nephew could not produce the blood money to absolve him from the murder of a member of another family, threw on the ground the exact sum, untouched, which that family had paid her grandfather as blood money, illustrates the persistence of the 'customary law'.

In all these frontier districts, the Afghan government had been trying gradually to replace a patchwork of different customs with a common law which did not sacrifice the element of true justice in the Jirgah system or so antagonize the local tribesmen that they ignored the courts and reverted to personal revenge. For a while the authorities had considerable success in this. One district governor told me that in his area, which included the villages of the fierce and hitherto unruly Mangals, there had been in the previous five years no murders and only one case of manslaughter (the accused was a child). This view was confirmed by the fact that in 1966, for example, I was permitted to travel in these tribal areas without any escort, though my party included two women. This would not have been the case a decade before, and under Daoud, until 1977 at least, the rule of law seems to have been still further tightened.

A number of factors contributed to this acceptance of central and common control. In the first place, it was administered by those who, like the tribesmen themselves, were fighting men – that is to say, by the Afghan army. Then again, central authority clearly brought with it a number of material improvements – in agricultural techniques, communication, medicine and education – so that the new ways as a whole were gradually identified as beneficial. Finally, the tribal Jirgah was not suddenly deprived of power and influence, but rather had its function changed to that of a local government council concerning itself with local construction and irrigation projects, and with disputes over property, the use of irrigation water, and so on.

This is not to say that nationally administered law was completely accepted by all except a criminal class. The administrative arm of the law still did not stretch into every corner of the country. But events like those following the case in Badakshan in 1964, when three Germans were shot by local villagers (one of the Germans, left for dead, photographed the assassins, made his way back to Kabul and developed the picture which led to the capture and execution of the murderers), slowly created a general recognition of the rule of a central and common law.

The acceptance of fairly wholesale changes in laws and customs does not in the long run depend on any abstract intellectual acceptance of their appositeness. Acceptance depends on their being seen as part of a general evolution which is beneficial. The most obvious measure of the beneficence or otherwise of that evolution is in its ability to improve material standards, but no improvement in standard of living would be acceptable to most Afghans if it were achieved at the price of freedom. The increasing arbitrariness of Daoud's régime exacerbated the suspicion and hostility of the mullahs whose privileges were primarily at risk. By the time Taraki's PDP seized power much of the ground won in the 60s and early 70s had been lost, with local people acquiescing sullenly in the military imposition of central authority when it could not be escaped or resisted, and reverting to local traditional codes and authorities as soon as the military back was turned.

5 THE PIPER'S PRICE

Four-fifths of Afghanistan, a country three times the size of England and Wales, is desert, yet four-fifths of the population earns its living from agriculture or the cottage industries and crafts associated with it. The deserts or semi-deserts are not all immutable, and many of them in the west and south-west of the country were once highly fertile irrigated areas. Although not as easily as was once hoped, they can be rendered fertile again by the waters of those deserts of snow and ice high in the Afghan mountain ranges. All in all, about two-thirds of the land yields some kind of grazing, however sparse and seasonal. In much of Afghanistan there is good soil but no water, while often where there is water the soil is poor or non-existent. The basic problem for Afghanistan is to mate soil and water to fertility. It is a problem which has been clearly recognized by successive Afghan governments since the 1950s and some progress in the development of the irrigation and hydro-electric power has been made. There are about 3.5 million to 4 million hectares under irrigation, a third of the cultivatable land. A quarter of the irrigated land lies fallow each year. Linked to the major irrigation schemes is hydro-electric generation which accounts for 80% of Afghanistan's 318 megawatts capacity. This is only half utilized and while it brings electricity to nearly all the main towns, is not primarily for domestic use − this facility being enjoyed, like the piped water supply, by only 5% of the population. This problem of bringing water to the land is a major preoccupation at every level, from those who seek to dam the Oxus, the Helmand and the Hari Rud and use their waters for large scale irrigation, to the peasant who is trying to divert the water of a passing mountain stream to a few square yards of land.

Some years ago an elderly Pathan, steel-rimmed spectacles perched authoritatively on the end of his nose, accosted me one morning as we made breakfast camp in Paktya. His problem and his solution were typical – as was his belief that, since I was a European, I must be an engineer. He wanted to raise water some six or eight feet from the small river which flowed twenty yards from his land to irrigate a bare patch about the size of a tennis court. He had brought with him a couple of dozen neighbours (typically willing to join in a voluntary co-operative effort of this kind), and he hoped, by piling boulders across the river opposite the top end of his field, to divert sufficient water to it. However, even he had slight doubts about the feasibility of this. The river was swift but shallow, and at that point the water would have had to be raised considerably; yet in debouching from a gorge higher up it made a shallower dam further upstream impossible. It was at this juncture that he consulted one highly unqualified British 'engineer'. No hydro-dynamicist, it nevertheless occurred to me that, if only something as simple as a heavy concrete beam with the open ends of half a dozen plastic pipes embedded in it had been available, it might have been lodged in the fast moving river well above the point at which it was wanted and the water led by flexible pipe to the field as required. Such gadgets were not available and one could only talk about the best spot for the primitive boulder dam. We left our bespectacled friend noisily issuing orders to his neighbours to begin the work. I never knew if it achieved its object, but on its success or failure and on the success or failure of a thousand little enterprises like it, much depends for Afghanistan whose basic prosperity, despite attempts to industrialize in the past thirty years, must for a long time yet depend on improvement in agriculture.

About half the agricultural land is owned by the cultivator though part, if sometimes a large part, of his produce will usually be mortgaged to the local money lender. The average holding is 3 hectares, the vast majority of holdings falling in the range of 0.5 hectares to 6 hectares. Holdings under 20 hectares accounted for 60% of land ownership in 1967 and those over 100 hectares for 8%. In a prosperous area such as Paktya or Kunduz, for example, a 2 hectare holding of good, irrigated land would yield 3 tons of wheat and 2 tons of cotton. This would provide food for a family of six or seven and an income of 35,000 afghanis*, which compares favourably with a labourer's 15,000 afghanis a year or an industrial worker's 12,000 to 20,000 afghanis (see page 125). Yields vary greatly and that from a well-irrigated, fertilized area using improved seeds can be twenty times as high as that for traditional dry land wheat. Wheat yields rose 25% between 1968/9 and 1976/7 (other grains by 4% to 10%) making Afghanistan in normal times, with sensible reserve purchasing policies, self-sufficient in food. The

---

*The official exchange rate of afghanis early in 1980 was 72 to the £ and 31 to the dollar, but these rates were quite artificial, the real purchasing power might be more of the order of 116 to the £ and 50 to the dollar. Because of the favourable balance of trade achieved by large capital injections of foreign aid, the afghani has been a strong currency, its value improving from 80 to the dollar in 1972/3 to 43 to the dollar in 1977.

Soviet invasion, however, has had a catastrophic impact on spring planting, and the widespread starvation, particularly in the more remote and recalcitrant regions, which can be expected in the winter of 1980, will put another weapon in Soviet hands. The Russians will no doubt be quick to blame US refusal to sell *them* wheat for any difficulty they may have in supplying Afghanistan.

An important factor in a land of such fiercely independent people is that the peasant is able to be his own boss. However, many Afghan peasants operate some form of sharecropping rather than direct ownership, as the high cost of good land means that the ordinary landless peasant has no hope of saving enough to buy a viable plot. The Taraki régime's promise to limit holdings to 15 acres and distribute the rest to them must at first have seemed attractive. But there are in fact very few large landowners, other than the Wafqs, in Afghanistan, though there are many absentee landlords. One estimate in 1960 identified only thirty landlords with over 200 hectares. In any case, the peasants are usually so fatalistic and improvident that any redistribution of the land would be likely to be short-lived in the face of influential landowners' objection. On the other hand, the low level of mechanization – about three thousand tractors in the whole country – means the larger landlords are almost all forced of necessity either to hire labour additional to the family labour force or to allocate their land to other cultivators on a sharecropping basis.

It is just possible that the aspiring landowner might begin to make his money from freelancing in the timber trade. The hills in Paktya are an impressive sight, stretching for miles and miles with trees dotted over their entire surface, but rather sparsely, standing each three or four yards from its neighbour, the whole looking like a hesitantly gathering crowd. The timber in the past was haphazardly felled and cultivated scarcely at all, but in 1965 a group of West German forestry experts set up a major forestry project near Ali Khel to increase timber exports to Pakistan and try to halt the depletion of Afghanistan's 3% of forested land. There is already a steady, if unofficial, trade in camel-borne cedar baulks which fetch in Peshawar or Kohat three or four times what they can be sold for to the Kabul merchants.

Paktya is not, of course, the only prosperous agricultural area in Afghanistan. There is the now relatively successful development in the Helmand Valley; and the main areas for the cultivation of cotton — Afghanistan's chief cash crop — in Kataghan, round Mazar-i-Sharif and in the province of Kunduz are also agriculturally prosperous (Khanabad in Kunduz claims to be 'the seed gourd of Afghanistan'), as are the Herat and Jalalabad regions.

Yields are not high for most crops; wheat for example, despite American backed experiments with over three hundred different varieties, generally has a yield ratio between 6:1 and 12:1. Between 1953 and 1972 production increased in total from 2 million tons to only 2.4 million tons, an actual fall per head. The Afghan small farmer thinks in terms of subsistence only, for the motivation to produce surpluses or to go in for cash crops has not been strong enough. Most cash crops and such other money making agricultural lines as Karakul skins have been compulsorily purchased at fixed prices below their real value by the government. The major exception has been the development of cotton growing from a level of 60,000 tons in 1965 to an estimated 165,000 tons in 1976. Acreage was doubled but yields were also up 14% and parallel with this was an almost 400% increase in domestic cotton ginning.

It was on cotton processing that Afghanistan's industrial expansion principally relied in the 1960s and 70s with the establishment of gins, presses and oil-extraction and oil-processing plants. A major agent of this expansion was the Spinzar Company ('Spinzar' means white gold), a combination of private and state enterprise in which the controlling power now lies with the state. It was astonishing to see the transformation which a single enterprise such as this could bring to the remote towns and villages strung out along the Oxus. It is no exaggeration to claim that in this area, until recent times, virtually every hospital and most schools and housing projects were due to the stimulus or actual creation of the Spinzar Company. This should be remembered when considering the not overgenerous terms on which Spinzar employed its labour, or the conviction under Daoud's presidency of several of its directors and executives on charges of corruption.

The Afghan industrial worker works a six-day week and for his labour, the well-established but unskilled male worker receives from 40 to 70 afghanis a day, although he may start out on as little as 30 afghanis a day. In some cases he will also have access to free medical treatment and to subsidized industrial compound housing of above average quality. On the other hand, on one occasion in Khwaja-i-Gar during the democratic period, I was told that since a generator had broken down the factory gates had been locked, and the workers would not be paid for the days of enforced idleness. When I challenged the senior representatives of the company in Kunduz on this, they said that normal practice was to pay for lay-offs of this kind. The Afghan worker lacks effective or militant trade unions to take up his cause, although they would be perfectly legal under the constitution. Wages in fact are negotiated on an individual contract basis with no limit on hire or fire. A good man can, of course, negotiate himself into a relatively strong position, and a really top-line foreman, for example, might earn between 70 and 100 afghanis a day. This is more than is earned by most doctors or senior civil servants, either of whom might have to pay as much as 1,800 afghanis a month for a government-allocated and not necessarily superior house. A doctor's basic salary is 2,000 afghanis a month. A grade 4 (there are twelve grades) civil servant at deputy director level earns 4,200 afghanis a month. The weaker, less able worker, by contrast, may soon find himself dismissed – not that the arbitrariness is by any means all on the employer's side, for the Afghan industrial worker is prone to impulsive fits of absenteeism.

In 1967 there were scarcely a dozen factories in the western sense in the whole of Afghanistan. A sugar factory at Baghlan, a textile mill and a cement factory at Pul-i-Khumri, a porcelain pottery in Kunduz, the cotton-processing factories near Kandahar, a few small plants in Kabul – these provided the sole industrial opportunities in Afghanistan. (There were then probably less than ten thousand industrial workers in Afghanistan.) The equipment in these factories, although in many cases being replaced by new models from Russia and the West, was sometimes still of very ancient vintage. The soap-making in the Spinzar plant at Kunduz, for instance, was done with German equipment dating back to 1928.

Today there are some one hundred and thirty medium sized firms in Afghanistan, but as a result of Daoud's policies from 1973 onwards the manufacturing sector is dominated, and the mining sector monopolized, by the state. Only six new private manufacturing enterprises involving foreign participation, for example, were opened between 1973 and 1977. Eighty-six per cent of private sector investment is concentrated in Kabul. Ten of the twelve largest industrial enterprises are state owned and the other two in mixed ownership, and between them they account for over 60% of industrial employment. The average employment of the private firms is eighty people, with only five employing over two hundred. In all, the industrial and mining sector employs only forty-one thousand people, about one in eight of them women, which represents less than 1% of the work force as opposed to the 85% employed in agriculture and associated trades.

Even today, the Afghan industrial worker has no mass-production traditions behind him and is, in fact, just a retrained agricultural worker. He does not take easily to the disciplined regularity of modern industrial work, to the clocking in and out, and the necessity of keeping pace with a continuous production process. When harvest time comes round, as often as not he will down tools and dash back to the fields where he can earn for a few weeks as much as double his normal wage and all found. Harvest over, he is outside the factory gate again asking for his job back.

What kind of worker does the Afghan make, then, when he works? The answer probably lies somewhere between the assertion of the rather embittered West German engineer who claimed that the Afghans were quite unteachable and that even the technicians forgot everything they had ever learned when they got back from abroad, and the claim of the Afghan supervisor that his men were 'absolutely marvellous'. The more objective judgement of a Russian engineer in charge of cotton machinery installation to whom I spoke on one visit, was that they took much training but once trained were good workers. It seems to take about a year to train the quite ordinary semi-skilled worker in one of the cotton processing jobs, not because of any lack of native ability but through shortage of training facilities. The great bulk of the training, therefore, is of the on-the-job kind; and on-the-job training of illiterate peasants, using a variety of machines whose instructions are in any case printed in a number of different foreign languages, is not easy and is of necessity oral and slow. And yet, although in formal terms the Afghans have yet to show any outstanding aptitude for technology, they have a positive genius for mechanical improvisation. Vehicles are kept running which in Europe or America would long have rusted away on the scrap heap. They seem able to make do and mend almost indefinitely: a valuable asset in a country where spare parts are often unobtainable. It should not, therefore, prove too difficult to adapt this instinctive appreciation of mechanical functions to the more routine applications of industrial society.

The real problem is not one of techniques and training, of native ability or lack of it, but of attitude: the attitude – by no means confined to Afghanistan, a modern Briton must admit – of 'why work if there is a chance of getting rich quickly by speculation or gambling.' To the love of speculation must be added a positively Micawberish expection that something will turn up. The labour problem is essentially one of creating a new kind of social responsibility appropriate to a modern society, responsibility to the family, the village, the country. Opportunity for initiative and incentives for seizing it must be swiftly introduced to the ordinary man to remove what a former governor of Balkh described to me as 'a fatalistic satisfaction with the status quo'. Wishful thinking, centred on speculation and gambling, has to be removed and replaced by a desire to work if Afghanistan is to be industrialized. Whether the Afghan will be happier after such a change is a different matter.

But large-scale industrial activity is for the future; for

the present the vital considerations are the quantities of wheat, cotton and rice, Karakul skins, wool woven into carpets, and dried fruit which the country can produce to feed itself and for export.

Afghan carpets are famous. There is far more to their complex individual production than the weaving referred to in Chapter 4, although estimates as to the labour involved in this process vary from those given by the carpet makers on the spot in Chahardarra, to the official figure of four women weaving ten square metres of carpet in a month. Before the wools can be woven, they go through an elaborate process of vegetable dyeing; a host of wild herbs and flowers are available to produce the acid and alkaline dyes in all the many shades that go into the Afghan carpet. Just over half a million square metres of carpet are produced annually, and of this four-fifths are exported – principally to England and West Germany, often via Russia. The value of the carpets exported in 1975/6 was 16.1 million dollars.

Equally beautiful and almost as lucrative are the thousands of Karakul skins, or Persian Lambs, which find their way to Afghan heads and rich female shoulders all over the world. (The chief overseas market today is New York, which since the war has displaced London as the main outlet.) The skins – black, brown, grey, gold, and rarest of all, white – are of fine quality. The gold skins, with their infinite changes of shade and light, must surely be the inspiration for the Jason legend. Some ten million Karakul skins are sold abroad annually and fetch around 10 million dollars in export earnings. Golden fleeces indeed! The Karakul farmer does not perhaps gain his fair share of these rich rewards. The government has established a co-operative marketing system through which the skins are bought at a fixed price, according to grade, that is very substantially below the real market price. The purpose of this, it is claimed, is to assure the farmer of a regular outlet at a stable price for his skins under all circumstances, but clearly it is also designed to make money for the government. If the quality and quantity of Karakul skin production is to be maintained, the price to the farmer himself will have to be substantially increased in the next few years. The major agricultural exports, however, are cotton, (35 million dollars a year, mainly to the Soviet Union) and, largest contributor of all at 75 million dollars, the fruit one sees drying in the sun on the flat mud roofs of the Afghan villages and the fresh fruit and nuts that make summer and autumn travel in Afghanistan such a delight. The remaining cottage industries – leather working, sheepskin jackets, and the delightfully intricate pieces of hand-beaten copper – are important mainly for saving scarce foreign currency by supplying the domestic market. These essentially agricultural products are not easy to nurture in the harsh climate of Afghanistan. If the winter is too severe and late, it affects the Karakul lambs; if it is too mild and ends too early with little rain, then it fails to keep down the grubs which destroy the grass roots. If the herds and flocks are too small, there is not enough wool for the carpets; if they are too large and graze indiscriminately, then the earth is stripped bare and erosion sets in. If there are too few donkeys, then there is too little transport for what is grown; if there are too many donkeys, they destroy the vegetation. The need is for better husbandry, improved strains of seed and livestock and the development of the appropriate small-scale machinery, such as motorized hand tractors. In the past there have been too many generously given and totally useless normal farm tractors rusting in old forts, and even by the roadside, because they were far too large to use on the Afghan's typically small plot. All

(Top) The Russian engineered Salang tunnel, at 13,000 feet, enables the formidable Hindu Kush to be crossed at virtually all times of year. (Bottom) Some two million nomads add to both the volatility and colour of Afghan life. These are heading for their summer pastures in the hills of Badakshan, which even the might of the Soviet army seems unable to bring within its control.

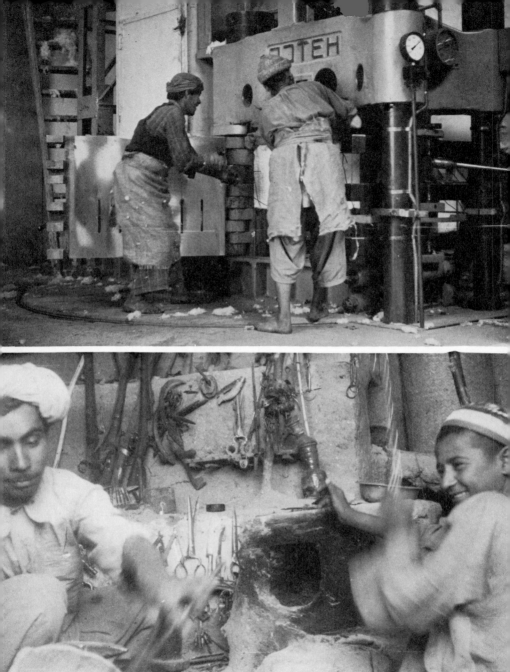

(Top) Russian machinery has come to replace much of the older western plant in many Afghan factories. (Bottom) The Afghan smith is adept at improvised repair and manufacture of everything from a Land Rover engine to a saucepan, a plough share to homemade ammunition.

(Top) Purdah at puberty was the rule for Afghan women until Daoud's decree of 1956 but even now is observed by the traditionalists. (Bottom) After Afghanistan's first elections to the Wolesi Jirgah, the four women deputies were well able to hold their own in argument with their male colleagues, as this picture taken outside the parliament building shows.

The obligations of Islam are strictly observed by the great majority of Afghans whether at the back of a crowded shop or, as here, in the isolated midst of a windswept desert.

these agricultural improvements require capital and the Afghan small farmer does not have it.

Striking it rich is the dream of every underdeveloped country hoping to solve all problems of capital for development. If not on a bonanza scale, two major discoveries in Afghanistan in the past few years bear rich promise for the future: natural gas at Shiberghan in the Balkh province, and iron-ore at Hajigak in Bamian. The gas reserves are estimated at 130 billion cubic metres and production varies between 2.6 billion cubic metres and 3 billion cubic metres, of which 95% is exported from Shiberghan to the Soviet Union at a value (1975/6) of 46.3 million dollars or some 20% of Afghanistan's exports. It was originally planned to lay a second pipeline south towards Hajigak, and along its route factories were to be established using the pipeline as a source of power. The first factory, a fertilizer plant in Mazar-i-Sharif itself, 110 kilometres from the gas source, produces 56,000 tons of fertilizer a year. It was supposed to be in production by 1967 but eventually came on stream in 1972. The terminus of this second pipeline was to have been in the Hajigak, for the phased development of a steel industry.

It was estimated by an Afghan survey that the iron-ore deposit at Hajigak amounts to 1,760 million tons of a very high grade (62% iron content is the official estimate). Moreover, only a few miles away there is a substantial deposit of limestone for use in iron-ore smelting. Despite the tempting juxtaposition of all the necessary ingredients, the present scale of Afghan industrial development, the limited prospects of export of steel to neighbouring countries, the inadequate development of the transport system for a large-scale export of iron-ore and the altitude of the deposits — 4,000 metres, all make the development of more than a small-scale steel industry imprudent. The real problem for this and all other gas-related development, however, is that the contract with Russia and the need to repay capital and interest on the massive Soviet loans has pre-empted all the gas supply.

Extensive traces of other mineral deposits have been found throughout Afghanistan. There is a large sulphur deposit near Nangarhar. Coal has been mined in small quantities in a dozen places for many years, but now recent surveys have revealed proven deposits of 100 million tons and an estimated further 400 million tons. Copper has also been discovered in substantial quantities at Ainak where deposits are estimated at 4.7 million tons metal equivalent. Lead, manganese, marble, gypsum, barite, gold, beryl and uranium have all been found.

As one might expect in this part of the world, oil has also been discovered but so far there has been nothing more encouraging than the eight to nine million tons estimated at Saripul and about three million tons elsewhere − far less than the reserves of the rich fields of Persia and southern Russia. One of the oldest mining operations in Afghanistan is for the semi-precious and very beautiful lapis lazuli found only in the remote mountain regions of Badakshan, where some of the mines are so high that they can only be worked in summer. Between thirty to forty tons of this ultramarine stone, shot through with threads of gold, are mined each year.

The development of all these mineral resources with just the right balance of proportion between them, will require a very sophisticated level of planning in a country where there are too few trained administrators and where both private and state capital are in short supply. The perennial failure to create indigenous capital has been the Achilles heel of the Afghan economy.

The traditional source of bootstrap capital is personal saving, but for the great majority of Afghan peasants and farmers it is simply not practicable to save. As one observer succinctly put it 'Should he use his income to improve his farm he would die of starvation.' The most common source of local finance is the money lender, usually a nomad or local landowner, but such borrowing is a last resort and to stave off an immediate crisis rather than to increase productivity or earning power.

To some extent central government can and does prime the pump but it, too, is faced with the problem of finding capital from inadequate sources, much of which is in any case earmarked for military expenditure*. As far as internal revenue raising is concerned, the government relies on three principal sources: customs duties and tolls, taxes on foreign currency earnings and a margin of profit on their compulsory exchange at below the market rate, and direct taxation of land, income and profits. This latter category of taxes only accounted for 20% of domestic revenue in 1966 and still only 22% in 1977 and even though Daoud's draconian tax gathering methods markedly improved the yield, it is a fair guess that less than half the sums due are actually paid in a country where it is extremely difficult to quantify either a man's capital or his revenue. The ratio of tax to GNP of

---

*It is, not surprisingly, impossible to arrive at a figure for military expenditure. I was able to do a calculation in 1966 which suggested a level of 1,200,000 afghanis a year or about 30% of government revenue and this would have accounted only for payments for personnel, buildings, maintenance, transport etc., since the bulk of the cost of weapons and equipment is met by the Soviet Union. Estimates for pre-invasion levels of expenditure suggest that this was still running at 25% to 30% on revenue items but capital expenditure, mainly in the form of Russian aid, is harder to estimate.

7% is almost the lowest in the world. The extraordinarily powerful landowners' lobby in the Wolesi Jirgah during the democratic decade ensured that no taxes inimical to its interest were voted (these included proposed vehicle and fuel taxes) and even in more recent and autocratic times it has been hard to overcome the resistance of this powerful group to taxation. Imported vehicles are now punitively taxed, i.e. 8,000 dollars on a two-litre car and 100% tax common on all vehicles. The result is that Afghanistan's sixty to seventy thousand buses, trucks and cars (fifty-one thousand in 1975) become increasingly ancient and dilapidated.

The land tax introduced in 1975 was levied on the basis of seven different grades of potential productivity, with holdings of 1 hectare exempt and those under 2 hectares having a 40% relief. The average 3 hectares holding of grade 1 quality land would pay 900 afghanis in tax. The typical 2 hectare landowner referred to before would pay only 450 afghanis on his 35,000 afghani revenue. He would pay additionally, on average, about 12% of his gross sales value in other taxes.

Customs duties, road tolls and other levies of this kind are largely evaded by an elaborate system of *baksheesh* – an Afghan frontier customs post often looks more like a living page from *Exchange and Mart* than an official tax point. As each lorry drives up it is approached by two men. The Customs Officer goes to the offside and enters into animated discussion with the driver on the nature and size of his load. A small sum for official dues may or may not change hands. Meanwhile on the passenger side the second man, often not even a customs man but a relative or friend of the man in charge of the post, also enters into an animated discussion as a result of which money or a melon, a cooking pot, a woven basket, or any one of a hundred other items is handed over and the lorry is waved imperiously on its way. In any case about a third of Afghanistan's trans-border trade does not even trouble to go through this charade but is smuggled in and out across literally thousands of unguarded, and often unguardable, trails, some of which even lead to the supposedly incorruptible Soviet Union. Narcotics agencies have suggested that since the closure of much of South-East Asia as a drugs supply source, drug smuggling from Afghanistan has greatly increased. Though this is vehemently denied by Afghan governments, it seems probable that part of the 'unaccounted' element in Afghanistan's foreign exchange surplus derives from this source. Customs duties are rendered even more insecure as a source of revenue by the propensity of Afghanistan's southern and western neighbours to close their borders when involved in a dispute with Kabul.

Taxes on foreign trade are more reliable and the fact that so large a part of Afghanistan's exports (40% to 50%) go to Russia, does avoid some of the risks associated with customs revenues. However, the bulk of such earnings is simply retained by the Soviet Union to meet debt and interest payments and never finds its way into the Afghan treasury, and the dependence on foreign trade taxes for three-quarters of government revenue cannot last. Apparent surpluses on foreign exchange transactions in fact conceal net losses, as purchase subsidies are 'lost' in general government expenditure. On the other hand, since 1974, there have been substantial remittances from the two hundred thousand Afghans employed abroad, mainly in Iran and the Gulf States. In 1972 domestic revenue was only 26% higher than it had been in 1939, but between then and 1976/7 it doubled and despite the current account deficit the large injection of foreign capital provided a healthy balance of payments surplus in the 1970s. Revenue in 1979/80 was

£377,000,000, but aid accounted for almost one-third of this.

Governments unable to increase the amount of money domestically available through taxation to carry out their plans, are unlikely to care much where revenue comes from, or to have much regard for social goals or even simple equity in framing their taxation policies.

In such difficult circumstances it is not surprising that the Afghan government relies for 80% of its development expenditure on foreign aid. We shall study the political implications of this in the next chapter, but its economic consequences have been almost as serious for Afghanistan. It has, for example, been a condition of many aid projects that some matching capital be provided from domestic sources. This has meant a heavy drain on available capital for which the private sector has to compete. In 1953, when the aid boom began, Afghanistan's public sector absorbed some 35% of total domestic credit, but by 1973, when Daoud next came to power, it already took 70%, a level rare outside the socialist economies, and continued to climb. The governments of the democratic decade acknowledged the lamentable failure of most public sector enterprises to contribute to development and made some rather half-hearted and unsuccessful attempts to reverse the process. They were unable, however, to abandon the Afghan belief in the virtues of central economic control — essential to such a reversal.

The funds made available through the banks, and Da Afghanistan Bank in particular, at compulsorily low rates of interest, were almost entirely taken up by official projects so the private sector had to turn to the bazaar, where interest rates were between 20% and 40% per annum. Fry estimated that 50% of agricultural and general trade capital and 30% of construction capital had to be found in this way. It is indicative of the resilience of the Afghan that even in such a climate most individual businessmen, until 1978 at least, were optimistic about their prospects.

Because of the Cold War game, Afghanistan has seldom experienced much difficulty in obtaining large sums of foreign aid – though seldom all of the astronomic sums demanded by its grandiose paper plans – plans which usually yield rather more modest achievements in practice. This has not only distorted the Afghan economy in practical terms, as Dupree has pointed out, but in my view much more seriously has distorted the attitude of Afghan governments to their economic problems. Many leading Afghans have acquired the belief that little or no effort is required of them and that they do not, either individually or collectively, have to modify their conduct or customs in any way to achieve economic development. The failure of enterprises undertaken in this spirit is almost inevitable. Foreign aid-funded projects seldom yield even sufficient return to service the debts incurred in launching them. For this the donors must share the blame. (Though since the aim in the Soviet case is to create dependence, Russia would not presumably regard this as blameworthy.) The Afghan's innate tendency to blame foreigners for all his ills comes conveniently to his rescue at this juncture. Thus is created a vicious circle in which indifference and incompetence has led to ever greater reliance on foreign aid, especially Soviet aid, which in turn has led to still greater indifference and incompetence.

The acid test of any economic policy must be whether or not the majority of the citizens are – or at least feel they are – better off as a result of it. Certainly in the

forty years from 1932 to 1972 real wages went up by between 70% and 156%. The same period saw wild fluc-
tuations in the rate of inflation. In the 1940s it averaged
well over 27%, in the 1950s it swung from 23% to a
deflationary rate of −15% and averaged out at only
some 3%, while in the 1960s the average was 10% but,
unlike the inflation rate in almost every other part of the
world, it held steady in the 1970s at about 6% per annum. These inflation figures, however, are based on urban prices and it is difficult to tell how accurately they
reflect the domestic financial vicissitudes of the majority
of Afghans.

Almost entirely as a result of massive injections of aid
− which have totalled well over seven billion dollars in
the past twenty-five years − GNP has gone up − but not
by nearly as much as it should have done following such
massive investment. In real terms it rose just over 30%
from 1950 to 1960, from 1960 to 1970 by 28% and from
1970 to 1977 by 27%. But now that most even remotely
justifiable infrastructure projects have been completed,
that growth must slow still more, even if peace is
restored. Nor in a country where so small a proportion
of the population work for cash wages can such yard-
sticks have much more than econometric significance.

The really crucial question is whether the ordinary
Afghan is better off. It is difficult to answer these questions in the absence of reliable statistics. A doctor will
speak of extensive malnutrition while the evidence of
one's eyes suggests that food is both good and relatively
cheap and plentiful. Kebabs and kormas with plenty of
meat, flat discs of coarse tasty bread and bowls of rice,
salt and spices, fruit from apricots to melons, high quality tomatoes and cucumbers − all seem plentiful. On the
other hand, the visual evidence of disease is also plen-

tiful. Half the children born do not live to their fifth birthday and life expectancy for the rest is still only fifty years. Rarely does one see an Afghan in rags, or the rows of sleeping beggars which are a common sight in such Asian cities as Calcutta, but the drainage and water supply are almost invariably unhygienic and inadequate, and your drink of water is more than likely to be brought to you in a fine copper cup filled from the *jui* (open ditch) which also serves as laundry and latrine.

Afghanistan is an incongruous blend of the old and the new, albeit one in which the old still predominates. It is a country suspended in a limbo between the Middle Ages and the twentieth century: purdah and green plastic sandals; cadillacs and Karakul skins; the host who will beggar himself in the name of hospitality, and the servant in the modern hotel who will drive you mad with his constant demands of *baksheesh*; the sophistication of supersonic jet fighters and the ancient creaking of a Cretan-style windmill pump; the imposing bulk of a massive hydro-electric scheme and the lines of *karez* or *qanat* holes dug down the hillside to irrigate a small patch of tired crops in some remote corner of the country. In all these antitheses the spectacular modern part has had but little effect on most Afghans. Afghanistan remains a country which is poor, though poor without that desperation which characterizes so many other underdeveloped countries. But the benefit of development has not been widespread. As a Nathan Institute report put it in 1972, 'Most Afghans can rightfully say that they are paying for the exclusive benefit of a privileged minority in privileged areas of the country.' It is on those sentiments that the revolutionaries of the past two years have tried to capitalize. But whoever holds power, major economic advance, and therefore the opportunity to spread its benefits to the people at large, will depend on large injections of foreign capital. This must now entirely hinge on Russia's willingness to supply it. That in turn will be determined solely by whether or not the Kremlin feels that the necessity of sending in Soviet forces has invalidated the policy of the past thirty years. The careful development of that policy is the subject of our next chapter.

6 RED TO MOVE

Despite King Amanullah's unsuccessful attempts to modernize his country, the commercial and industrial development of Afghanistan, in modern terms, did not begin until the 1930s. In 1933 Abdul Majid Zabuli, surely one of the most remarkable entrepreneurs of this century, founded the Bank Melli and through it a whole range of new industrial enterprises. His greatest stroke of genius lay in circumventing the Koranic prohibition against the charging of interest by inventing the 'money ticket'. By means of this the bank took a fixed 'profit' on its money and thus casuistically avoided the prohibition. Zabuli thus released the capital needed for development and the bank itself provided the funds for more than thirty enterprises from vehicle imports to hire purchase, electricity generation to cotton processing. In each of these the bank held a major and usually controlling interest, so that from the very outset the Afghan economy was based on the concept of centralized control of growth and development. It was not to matter what the political complexion of the government would be, royalist, as at this time, or pseudo-democratic or neo-socialist as it was to be in the 50s, 60s and 70s, this principle remained paramount. In fact, it was the arch capitalist Zabuli who introduced the concept of long term economic planning to Afghanistan in the early 30s.

Another characteristic of the Zabuli pre-war boom was the volume of trade with Russia; by the late 1930s this accounted for a third of Afghanistan's exports. World War II cut short both economic growth and, as a result of Russia's preoccupation with internal supply, the Soviet connection for neutral Afghanistan.

Once the war was over Zabuli, who had spent most of it comfortably installed in Switzerland, returned at the King's request to try and restore the country's fortunes. However, a new and much more significant factor had now entered the equation. From now on economic growth and economic and other ties with Russia were largely determined by the state of relations between Afghanistan and the new state of Pakistan over the Pushtunistan issue.

Although the United States dominated Afghanistan's external trade, aid and cultural contacts until 1953, the level of activity was at less than one million dollars a year. The turning point, almost unnoticed by a Britain trying to divest itself of an empire, a Europe rebuilding its shattered economy, and a United States concentrating on keeping Europe out of Communist hands, came in 1950.

In that year, as we saw in Chapter 3, following fierce exchanges on the border, Pakistan, through whose territory virtually all goods for Afghanistan had to pass, cut off its neighbour's petrol supplies. Russia immediately made a barter trade agreement with Afghanistan exchanging oil and textiles for wool and cotton.

During the 1950s the Americans were handicapped by their commitment to the ill-fated Helmand Valley project, begun as a contract between Morrison-Knudsen, a private American company, and the Afghan government. In the early 1950s the high walls of the M-K compound seemed to be symbolic of the shuttered attitude of its employees. The Helmand Valley project was certainly imaginative in conception, aiming as it did to restore fertility to a vast desert area south-west of Kandahar and to revive something of Afghanistan's claim to its ancient title of 'the granary of Central Asia'. But a number of snags, particularly the salinity of the irrigated area and the unforeseen social consequences of the new pattern of agricultural settlement which was required, meant that more and more capital had to be sent chasing the initial investment. The Americans did not feel that Afghanistan was ready for industrialization, so they confined their aid to the Helmand and other agricultural projects and to education and, because of wholly understandable preoccupations elsewhere, paid only scant and spasmodic attention to Afghanistan.

While the Russian commentator, R.T. Akhramovich, writing in 1966 about the immediate post-war stage of Afghanistan's economic development, was exaggerating when he claimed that 'developing Afghanistan, of course, did not find among her partners in the world capitalist market the slightest desire to co-operate in overcoming her economic difficulties,'[1] the West in general was certainly giving less attention than it should have to this strategically significant country. But America's dominant position in a neighbouring state was a cause of anxiety to the Soviet Union, at a time when the Cold War was at its chilliest and US Secretary of State Dulles was pursuing an aggressive foreign policy. That Russia feared that the wicked imperialists might pre-empt its own intentions in this part of the world is clear from Akhramovich's repeated accusations.

By linking up its national development programme with the imperialist monopolies, Afghanistan very soon found herself in the position of a debtor, and the prospects of realizing her plan proved to be completely dependent on foreign monopolies.

The US monopolists pressed these agreements on Afghanistan regarding them as a means of penetrating that country's economy.

US capital by controlling roughly half of Afghanistan's exports, forced on her the contract thus making sure of getting a good part of Afghanistan's foreign currency receipts.[2]

Fortunately for Russian ambitions, Prince Daoud became Prime Minister in 1953 and immediately embarked on those policies which were, unintentionally, to put Afghanistan under the paw of the bear. A fanatical Pathan, he hotted up the Pushtunistan dispute and partly at least from resentment at the fact that Bank Melli had made the bulk of its investment in the non-Pathan North, stripped the main driving force of the free enterprise Afghan economy of much of its power and investment control. He also played with zeal and some skill the Cold War game of setting the two great powers to compete in giving aid. By 1955 US aid was running at some two million dollars a year, and Russian post-war aid totalling twelve million dollars had by then reached about half the level of the US contribution. But Russia was already deploying its investment with great propaganda, skill and perhaps less regard for Afghanistan's real interests, though to be fair its emphasis on smaller scale agricultural investment was valid in economic terms. Early projects, such as paving the roads of Kabul, building grain silos in which US gift wheat was stored as if it came from Russia, and the construction of huge public bakeries, all made a good impact in the capital where the decisions on future commitments would be taken. That these projects had no effect on the needier provinces, that in due course the asphalt cracked and the bread lacked flavour, did not really matter.

In 1955 trouble broke out again over Pushtunistan and the Soviet Union launched a major drive to gain the dominant position in the Afghan economy. It entered into a trade agreement which enabled Afghan goods, and particularly the then crucial export of Karakul skins to New York and London, to escape Pakistan's blockade. By the end of the year Russia was buying some 20% of Afghan exports and, more importantly, had made its largest ever loan (one hundred million dollars) outside the socialist bloc at 2% over forty to fifty years – but it *was* a loan, not a grant. The Afghans got the full 'B & K circus' treatment in a state visit in that year, designed to show that Russia was anti-colonial, peace-loving and sympathetic. Khrushchev was at his table-banging best as he castigated 'the criminal policy of the colonialists whose long years of rule in those countries cause the people tremendous damage and greatly hinder their economic development.' He was particularly forthright in his support of Afghanistan over Pushtunistan.

At the same time the two countries entered into a new friendship treaty which, while it was basically an extension of earlier treaties, edged a little nearer to the kind of arrangement which the Russians were to make in December 1978 and to exploit in December 1979. It did seem at the time to offer security from direct invasion for anyone willing to believe Soviet promises and Bulganin made all the right noises. 'In its relations with Afghanistan the Soviet Union will continue to be guided by the principles of respect for territorial integrity and sovereignty, non-aggression, [and] non-interference in internal affairs. . . . ' (It is an amusing sidelight on the ephemeral hagiography of communist Russia that Akhramovich, writing after the disgrace of B and K, describes this and their subsequent state visit in 1960 as 'by a Soviet delegation'!)

Even then the situation could still have been retrieved by the western powers. In my view, Daoud was only ever pro-Soviet in so far as that stance was pro-Afghan. Soviet influence at that time was still purely economic and Daoud was seeking economic aid from all sources to *avoid* a situation where Russian influence would also become political and military. As he said at the time, 'If development is slow, poverty itself is a hotbed where communism or socialism might grow and prosper.' Indeed in 1956 it was to America that he first turned for military help and, it is rumoured, for a secret guarantee of his borders as well. However, America, as a member of SEATO and the Baghdad Pact, opted to support fellow member Pakistan in the Pushtunistan dispute and refused the Afghan request. Daoud was now genuinely concerned about the balance of power in the region, for not only was he in a state little short of war with the well-equipped Pakistan army on his south-eastern frontier, but at odds with Iran over boundaries and water in the south-west. The anti-imperialist conditioned reflex by which America automatically repudiated former British assessments in areas where the US was called on to fill the vacuum left by the withdrawal of British imperial power, thus drove Afghanistan further into the Russian sphere of influence.

Military aid has usually been the main goal of Russian economic penetration in the third world because of the virtual inevitability of military coups or military backing for communist inspired coups. In 1956 Russia made a twenty-five million dollar arms deal with Afghanistan to supply relatively modern tanks, aircraft and other technical aid. More significantly it began that arrangement for the training of Afghan officers, technicians and specialists which, by the time of the 1979 invasion, had processed some ten thousand men, or about 10% of Afghanistan's servicemen.

A few hundred Afghans, mainly pilots, have received their military training in the US and towards the end of his presidency Daoud tried to loosen the Soviet grip by sending more officers to India. He also tried to broaden the base of military allegiance by introducing non-Pathans into the officer corps (not something he would have considered during his premiership) and to create a second power base by building a large quasi-security police force. This he did by setting up a special police college to take on the best of the many thousand Kabul University graduates who left each year without jobs to go to. But these were the very students among whom the PDP, Afghanistan's Marxist organization, had been recruiting so diligently.

From the outset Russia kept a tight logistic grip on all the Afghan forces, deliberately restricting the supply of spares, fuel and ammunition, so that they would swiftly be rendered impotent if they chose to act against Soviet interest. The Afghan air force, for example, has never had more than enough fuel in hand for ten to fourteen days' operations and diesel for tanks was doled out in similar penny packets. My own conversations in peace time with Afghan officers and the view of shrewd observers of the military scene, suggested that while Afghan aircraft could quickly be grounded, the Afghan spirit of independence was less easily earthbound. As so often happens, the great majority of Afghans exposed to the culture shock of life in Russia (or America for that matter) became more deeply attached to their own national prejudices rather than won over to the official philosophy of their hosts. Nevertheless, a few were seduced and a number of the young lieutenants and captains of the 1960s became the impatient middle aged revolutionaries who held key staff and regimental positions when the time came for the Afghan Marxists to strike in 1978.

In 1957 the Soviet Union entered into an agreement with Afghanistan in which they funded an oil exploration team which found some quite substantial deposits (e.g. one field of the order of 500 million barrels) and gas deposits of more than 22 billion cubic metres, which, however, it took a considerable time to exploit and whose output was committed in advance at a fixed price to the Soviet Union – the only market available.

Nevertheless, economically, Afghanistan was still in a position of relative independence. In 1956 Afghan/Soviet trade balanced out at some 17 million dollars in each direction. But by the end of Daoud's first period of rule in 1963 the Soviet Union was exporting 72.5 million dollars worth of goods to Afghanistan but importing only 23 million dollars. The heavy, unfavourable balance of trade into which Afghanistan had largely been tempted by the credit terms offered (and of which the Russians had been so critical when such a position was enjoyed by the Americans) thus became an additional means of controlling the Afghan economy, though once natural gas came on stream this imbalance was redressed.

As early as January 1960 a Mangal tribal leader fleeing from retribution in Afghanistan to Pakistan could say 'the crux of the matter is that the Afghan government has taken strong exception to our objection to the growing Russian influence in Afghanistan, to giving the country into the iron grip of communists who are preaching their atheistic creed under one garb or another'.[3] This may well have been an excuse for 'a little local difficulty', but it is interesting that it could be considered even then as an excuse for the difficulty.

It is doubtful if Russia would have so swiftly achieved this position of dominance but for the renewal of the dispute over Pushtunistan from 1961 to 1963, which erupted into open conflict and brought legitimate transit trade, including the materials required for American aid projects, to a standstill for two years. In 1962 the two great powers tried to help Afghanistan by airlifts of its important fruit harvest. America provided, free, ten cargo flights a week to India for forty weeks. In the same period Russia mounted fifteen flights a day, almost all to the Soviet Union, and for which the Afghans ultimately had to pay. It was this third Pushtunistan dispute and its economic consequences which brought about Daoud's fall from power and the advent of a more democratic style of government by Prime Ministers such as Yusuf and Maiwandwal, sympathetic to the West. But, although America continued to step up its aid considerably and other western countries such as West Germany came substantially into the picture (even China gave aid of two million dollars) the battle was virtually over, though the Russians were careful to blow no premature trumpet blast of victory. Writing in 1968 about the peaceful competition between the two powers in his country, an Afghan economist living in the States could describe with equanimity a situation in which

> The Russians built the terminal building of Kabul Airport while the Americans supplied and supervised the communications system in the control tower. The majority of the trucks, automobiles and buses in Kabul are American made and yet all of them are run with Russian gasoline. It is in Afghanistan that one finds American automobilies driven on Russian paved streets, American wheat used in Russian made flour mills, Russian MiGs flown by Amer-

ican trained Afghan pilots and American cigarettes lit by Russian matches.[4]

My own favourite example was at Dilaram — Hearts Ease — where the Russians had just finished building a road over a bridge I had watched an American construct ten years earlier.

By 1968 Afghanistan had received more than twice as much Soviet aid as American; 550 million dollars to 250 million dollars. Eighty percent of the US aid had been in the form of outright grant, whereas two-thirds of the Soviet contribution was in the form of loans. These admittedly were long term at low interest and could be repaid in either commodities or Afghan currency, but the commodities were always valued by the Russians (and usually at less than originally agreed on grounds of poor quality) and the artificially high exchange rate with the rouble, which helped Afghanistan buy Soviet products, made repayment in local currency burdensome.

American efforts were concentrated on transport, which accounted for 40% of US aid. This was spent mainly on road building in the south, but also involved such white elephants as the largely unused Kandahar Airport. The second highest expenditure was on the wretched Helmand Valley project (22%) where yields were for a long time lower than they had been before the project. With glee, Akhramovich could write 'a telling blow was dealt to the prestige of the American "friends" for from behind the cloak of "assistance" the public saw the hated visage of colonialism which was threatening Afghanistan's independence.' America's generous supply of wheat (17%) went largely unnoticed by the general public in Afghanistan, though without it many people might have starved. Perhaps the most effective element of the American effort, though it comprised only 9% of the total, was in education, particularly teacher training, so much so that it drew Akhramovich's special condemnation. 'The US monopolists, like their partners in Western Europe, have considerably stepped up their penetration into Afghanistan under the guise of cultural assistance. Special attention has been given to education.'[5]

Soviet policy was to take advantage of every Afghan dispute with Pakistan to get the country more deeply into debt using techniques not unlike those of the rural money lenders they condemned. Fixed price contracts for purchase of commodities would be entered into at above world prices, but on such terms that long after the world price had risen above the agreed level Russia enjoyed the advantage. The Soviet Union would, it was true, take goods, such as poor quality Afghan wool, which no one else wanted, and supply commodities such as petrol, green tea, sugar, books and vehicles at below world prices. But it was noticeable that after 1963 Soviet trade agreements involved the sale to Afghanistan of such luxuries as cars, watches and cameras, the pursuit of which superfluities further strained the economy. They also included many more long term infrastructure projects which Afghanistan's state of economic development scarcely justified, but which often had strategic and political advantages for the Soviet Union. The classic example was the road building programme which was not designed to the advantage of the Afghan economy.

Nineteenth-century British strategists, concerned to keep Afghanistan an impenetrable buffer state, often warned grimly against the construction of a road south from Herat to Kandahar, for this would outflank the Hindu Kush. Today, you can drive in five or six hours between these two cities on a Russian built concrete highway, striking boldly across the brick red desert. Babur, the great Mogul, once struggled to stay alive in the deadly cold of a pass in the Hindu Kush by crouching in the corpse of an eviscerated camel. Now all the year round you can drive through the heart of these formidable mountains along the Russian built pass and tunnel at Salang, or fly over them in the aircraft of Aeroflot Ariana and Bakhtar – and at prices considerably below those of the international commercial airlines.

A glance at Map 4 (page 86) will show that the only good roads in Afghanistan are those which are part of the system completed in 1966, mainly by the Russians. This system is shaped like the Russian letter Ц. Its lines of communication run from the Soviet border north of Herat, through the major towns of Afghanistan (with the base of the Ц thoughtfully provided by the Americans) and back to the Russian border at the Oxus port of Qizil Qala. The tail of the Ц runs down to the Khyber, where there is access – via Peshawar and Karachi – to the sea. Transit trade agreements between Afghanistan and Pakistan allowed Russian goods, if not Russian guns, to roll unimpeded down to the Indian Ocean 'in fulfilment of historic destiny.'

This triumph for Soviet diplomacy tends to be overlooked in the West when discussing the Russian invasion little more than a decade later. In terms of that economic competition which is the corollary – often ignored in the West but never by the Russians – of peaceful coexistence, access to a warm-water port within easy reach of the seaboards of Africa and South Asia, and through which its goods can strategically be despatched, is as important to the Soviet Union as it was to tzarist Russia. Once the route was opened, the Russians had an even greater interest than had the government of British India in the stability of Afghanistan and in friendly relations across the Durand Line.

In the 1960s the Russian presence if inescapable, was discreet and sometimes exhibited an almost psychotic sensitivity to the presence of curious western visitors in Afghanistan. At this time the visitor to Qizil Qala, for example, however eminent the authority for his visit, would have found at his elbow, as I did, within moments of entering the dock area, a large blond Russian who claimed to be — and probably was — a maintenance engineer, but whose only discernible function seemed to be maintenance of a close watch on the visitor until safely out of the gate. All along the far bank of the Oxus there are squat gantry-legged observation posts even in peace time. The visitor with a camera who stands for more than a moment on the Afghan bank may find himself the centre of a diplomatic protest sparked off by a telephone call before his return to Kabul. Although no one seemed to object in 1966 to my taking photographs at Ay Khanum on the junction of the Oxus and Kochak rivers, this area — site of one of the great archaeological discoveries of modern times — was very difficult to visit,* even under the monarchy.

---

*The Hellenic site of Ay Khanum is remarkable almost as much for the way it was discovered as for what it contains. The King of Afghanistan, an ardent huntsman and a keen student of his country's history, was out hunting one day in 1963 along the Kochak river where it joins the Oxus. He came upon two unusual stones protruding from the ground: a Corinthian capital and an altar. He made no delay in getting these to the museum at Kunduz and in drawing them to the attention of the head of the French archaeological expedition, Dr. Schlumberger. The early excavations conducted by the new head of the mission, M. Paul Bernard, have revealed at Ay Khanum the first complete Hellenic city east of Mesopotamia. Ay Khanum was probably built in the second or third centuries BC in the wake of Alexander the Great's conquest. The city and its hilltop fortress oc-

Russia has often markedly underbid when tendering for major construction work in order to secure the contract, only to charge two or three times the estimate at the end of the day. This was particularly true in hydro-electric work where the Russians were anxious to elbow out the very successful West Germans. Soviet technical performance was sometimes not up to scratch either, but by the time disillusioned Afghans realized that their Marxist neighbours could deal as sharply as any western capitalists they were too deeply in hock to do much about it.

By the time Daoud seized power for the second time in 1973, Soviet aid at 1,500 million dollars between 1953 and 1973 was more than three times that of America (450 million dollars) and there were probably some three to four thousand Russian technicians working at all levels in Afghanistan. As Dupree wrote at the time of the coup:

> Afghanistan's economic problems are nothing new, but have been growing since the advent of overkill in foreign aid, which reached its peak during the 1953–63 decade of Daoud Khan's previous tenure. No matter how one viewed Afghanistan's economic problems, the outlook at first glance certainly appeared bleak. With most major infrastructure projects completed, with few real resources capable of earning vast sums of hard currency, with smug-

---

cupy a commanding strategic position with strong natural defences. There is evidence both *in situ* and in documentary sources to suggest that it was probably sacked and burnt to the ground towards the end of the second century BC by a tribe of nomads, the Urchi, from higher up the Oxus. Excited interest in the site, however, has to contend with 'difficulties' in reaching it. The author went there without asking; this, luckily, avoided the 'difficulties'.

gling and corruption steadily eroding income from customs
(a major source of government revenue), with little statis-
tical data for intelligent planning, with minimal overall in-
creases in agricultural production (and two years of
drought, disastrous to men, livestock, and crops), with
small success in attempted fiscal reforms, with debt repayment on foreign loans coming due, with annual budget def-
icits of about 500 million afghanis, with few of the country's
limited industrial and power plants operating at 50% capacity, with a bureaucracy oriented toward perpetuation rather
than innovation, Afghanistan offered any economist – free
enterprise, socialist, or mixed – extreme challanges.[6]

As was to be expected, the return to Kabul of an apparently sympathetic régime led to still further Soviet involvement in the Afghan economy. By the end of 1975
more than seventy new projects had been signed up, including major extensions of hydro-electric and irrigation
schemes, particularly in the tribally important (and still
[June 1980] untamed) Jalalabad region, development of
fertilizer production and the expansion of natural gas
production so that 2.5 billion cubic feet per annum
could be exported to the USSR from 1976. There were
the inevitable catches by which the Russians fixed the
prices, measured the quantities and pronounced unchal-
lengably on the quality of the goods exported. Athough
between 1973 and 1976 Russia increased the price per
thousand cubic metres of gas from 6.08 dollars to 16.1
dollars – in 1977 equivalent to 0.61 dollars per btu –
this has to be seen against a world price range of 0.60
dollars to 1.45 dollars per btu. By 1978, though aid at
400 million dollars for the year made Afghanistan the
fourth biggest recipient of Soviet bounty in total and the
largest per head of population, more than 40% of
Afghanistan's exports, including all its gas, were going to

pay off its debts to the Soviet Union. In imitation of the Soviet model Daoud had nationalized existing industries and directed a disproportionate amount of Afghanistan's scarce capital to further industrialization. He was, however, both an able man and a patriot. By 1975/6 he had begun to reassess his economic strategy and the implications of too close ties with Russia (as he did in other spheres). Moscow, detecting a change in attitude, became both less enthusiastic and less generous in its support. Counter-measures by the West were few and America diminished its economic and military commitment to the area, and particularly to Pakistan, when that country, in response to India's detonation of a nuclear bomb in 1974, began to pursue its own independent development of nuclear weapons with the aid of France. The completion of the Karakoram Highway linking Pakistan to China, marked the end of a process which had begun with the collapse of SEATO, the Baghdad Pact and the Bhutto régime and which divorced Pakistan from western interests. Such minor belated moves as the Iranian/Afghan transit trade agreement of 1974 could have little influence on the great game which Russia appeared to have won.

The Soviet Union had seen Afghanistan as a classical opportunity to prove that a society could be changed in a Marxist direction by economic penetration and the social impact of new technology. It was an artificially created state whose people had bitter memories of western imperialism. There was a largely poor, non-literate population and a great gulf between a small wealthy élite ruling group and the mass of the population. There was a rising and frustrated number of technocrats and students and a varied and mutually antipathetic racial mixture. There was a border with Pakistan in a continual state of dispute over the Pushtunistan issue and a strong central government and military organization largely dependent for its effectiveness on Soviet support. The Soviet Union, in other words, appeared to be running a highly successful experiment in economic penetration as a means of achieving political objectives and in the bountiful reward of neutrality as a means of encouraging other third world countries not to be drawn into the western camp.

Making due allowance for cant, the coincidental protestations of Russian commentators had a certain ring of conviction about them. As Akhramovich wrote 'regardless of the obvious facts, they, the apologists of British colonialism, kept propagating the idea that Afghanistan was threatened by "a fatal danger" from the North. . . . The selfless and friendly support of the socialist countries, by their very nature are far removed from any designs that might threaten the Afghan state.'[7]

Since in the 1960s and early 1970s Russia appeared to be content to ignore political principles and to help a neutral country ruled by a monarchy, where the Communist Party was actually illegal, in order to secure its long term advantages, the optimistic speculation of an Afghan commentator of the time seemed not unreasonable.

> Looking at the Soviet intentions in Afghanistan one could reasonably rule out a direct Soviet invasion of Afghanistan. In addition to the fact that the Afghans would defend themselves directly and through guerrilla war, the Soviet Union would lose the confidence of other neutral nations. She would suffer from world popular pressures and about 300 million Moslems of Asia and the Middle East would turn against her.[8]

That was certainly a view shared by most commentators, myself included, at the time and it was a view that appeared to hold good at least until very shortly before the coup which overthrew Daoud in April 1978. To understand what so dramatically changed the picture it is necessary to retrace the development of a number of political forces in Afghanistan.

7 EXPERIMENTS IN DEMOCRACY

In the heady atmosphere after World War II when so many underdeveloped nations either achieved or demanded their independence, in the sacred, if much abused, name of democracy, Afghanistan indulged in its first mild and brief flirtation with that siren. Dupree aptly named the preceding two decades the 'avuncular period' when government was almost entirely in the hands of members of the royal family. The pattern changed in 1950 with the law permitting some freedom in what had hitherto been a state press monopoly. Three main papers appeared which, while critical of the government and, in the context of 1950 Afghanistan, radical, were not revolutionary. Nor, of course, in an almost totally illiterate country did their circulation exceed a few hundred copies. Probably the most significant of them was *Afghan Mellat*, round which an informal national democratic socialist group coalesced. This group was in fact vehemently orthodox and irredentist over the issue of Pushtunistan. At the same time a student union was formed which naturally took an enthusiastic and iconoclastic interest in Afghan politics. The students' criticism, and that of the more left wing papers, particularly of the corruption of members of the government and of the reactionary influence of Islam, became increasingly virulent. After an abortive attempt to form its own political party to counter these critical organizations, the royal government reverted to type. In 1951 the students' union was closed and a few of its apprehensive leaders fled to Pakistan. By the end of 1952 all non-government papers had been closed and some twenty-five 'liberal' leaders were sent to prison, where some of them died. The first taste of democracy had not been to the liking of the ruling establishment, but although in 1953 the strong man of Afghanistan, Prince Daoud, had become Prime Minister, the appetite of many intellectuals for the power denied to them by the nepotism of Afghan politics, had been whetted.

The decade of Daoud's first period of rule will be considered elsewhere, but in examining the political development of Afghanistan it is significant in two respects.

In ten years Daoud enormously increased the grip of central government on Afghanistan at the expense of local rule and customs. Not since Abdur Rahman had an Afghan leader so effectively insisted that the writ of central government be paramount. Like his illustrious predecessor, he created a loyal, well-paid, well-trained army and used it, not only to govern the tribal districts, but to enforce the law generally. It had been customary, for example, for the wealthier citizens of Kandahar to neglect to pay their taxes, proffering excuses in their stead year after year to governments which had no choice but to accept them. In 1959 they tried their usual ploy — sanctuary in the mosque for a few days until the tax collectors got bored and went home — only to find their road to the mosque barred by Daoud's troops. Immediately they instigated a riot, but Daoud's commander was not impressed and simply shot some of the rioters. From thereon the taxes were paid.

This same willingness to exercise authority enabled Daoud to make reforms which would have been quite beyond the power of any progressive elements at that time. Again in 1959, on Daoud's initiative, a number of leading Afghan women abandoned purdah and its most public symbol the *chadur* or veil. The mullahs, ever quick to counter any threat to their absolute authority, sent a noisy deputation to protest to Daoud. After fifty of them had spent a week in jail they acquiesced to the new reform.

To carry out his economic and social programme Daoud needed resouces beyond those Afghanistan could supply and so he began that process which was to put the Afghan economy in pawn to the Soviet Union and which, unfairly in my view, earned him the sobriquet of 'the red premier' from the Americans whose aid, though substantial, was no match for Russia's. By 1963 there was widespread, if relatively peaceful, unrest at Daoud's leftward tilt in the balance of Afghanistan's neutral stance and against his social and economic reforms. It is more than likely that his influence in the armed services could have enabled him to stage a coup even then, as it did a decade later. However, in a remarkable gesture of self-denial, he stepped down from office at the King's request and there slowly began Afghanistan's second experiment in democracy.

Within a decade the experiment had failed – largely from lack of courage by the man who launched it. In 1964 Muhammad Zahir Shah, the King, deliberately abandoned two hundred years of autocratic rule and diminished his own personal power in order to give his country a system of government which could survive, as an absolute monarchy could not, the stress of the twentieth century.

The new constitution, which Zahir had a major hand in drafting, came into operation in 1965 following Afghanistan's first elections and imposed some surprising and shrewd restraints on the exercise of power. In particular, it barred the royal family from both politics and government, thus imposing on the recently ousted Prince Daoud perpetual exile from the legitimate exercise of power and closing the back door of quasi-constitutional usurpation to any possibly dissident relatives. It also set up a representative system of government formed by the Shura (parliament) consisting of the directly elected Wolesi Jirgah (House of the People) and the partly elected and partly appointed Meshrano Jirgah (House of the Elders). The older institution of the Loya Jirgah (Great Council) was composed of members of both houses of the Shura and the chairmen of elected provincial councils. The Loya Jirgah's functions were partly formal and partly to act as the sounding board of national opinion in times of great stress, such as a royal abdication or a state of emergency.

In promulgating this new constitution, the King seemed to be deliberately effacing himself and minimizing his power. An exquisitely well-mannered, highly civilized man, he was more interested in the culture and history of his country and in open-air sports than in the practice of government and the exercise of power. Yet he had a very real love of his country, and wisdom enough to know that the absolute authority of his family would ultimately be an obstacle to Afghanistan's progress.

As events were to prove, it was a mistake to look on the new constitution as a total abdication of the royal authority. Certainly, it imposed conditions and restraints: the King must be an Afghan national and, in effect, of the House of Nadir Shah; he must be a Muslim and a follower of the 'Hanafi doctrine'. But he also retained extensive reserve powers. Among royal prerogatives were the dissolution and summoning of the Shura, the appointment of the Prime Minister and other ministers, and of the Chief Justice and senior civil and military officials, and the proclamation of a state of emergency. It is true that the King was supposed to govern within the limits of the constitution, but that same constitution insisted that 'the King is not accountable and shall be respected by all.'

The restrictions on the political role of members of the royal family other than the King, have to be seen in the context of Afghan history, in which the most likely suspects in any plot against the King's life were his nearest, though not necessarily his dearest. It is only fifty years since a younger son outplayed and outfought his elder brother for the succession; only forty years since an Afghan monarch, Nadir Shah himself – so frequently styled 'martyr' in the 1964 constitution – was assassinated. The constitution's caution was no more than realism demanded. The problem of the succession is always a delicate one in an autocratic system, whether the autocracy be regal or 'proletarian'. It is at the death of the ruler that the state is most prone to upheaval and to the chaos that accompanies any prolonged struggle for power among aspiring heirs. The new Afghan constitution went into considerable detail in setting out the line of succession in the royal house and the conduct of any necessary regency. Particularly significant was the provision by which no one who had acted as permanent regent could subsequently become King himself.

Two factors were critical if the experiment was to succeed: self-restraint by the monarch and members of the royal house and the increasing derivation of government authority from the popular will, rather than from the whims of its appointed members. Whether such democracy is in fact the most beneficent form of government for a country such as Afghanistan is another matter. The issue was scarcely put to the test as both the critical elements for success were missing.

The Wolesi Jirgah was to be directly elected every four years by the universal suffrage of all Afghans over the age of twenty. (We shall see later how these elections were conducted.) It consisted of 216 members representing single member constituencies and was elected by the single direct vote system as practised, for example, in Britain. The Wolesi Jirgah could, therefore, have become as truly representative as any parliament elected by this rather crude method can ever be. Of the eighty-four members of the Meshrano Jirgah, one-third were directly elected every four years from constituencies coextensive with the twenty-eight provinces, one-third were representatives elected every three years by provincial councils to which they had previously been directly elected, and one-third were members appointed every five years by the King 'from amongst well-informed and experienced persons'. Thus, the composition of both houses of the Shura, and of the Loya Jirgah as well, was predominantly democratic, with members answerable to the voters at regular intervals.

At the first of these elections in the autumn of 1965 there were 1,358 candidates for the 216 seats in the Wolesi Jirgah (six of which were reserved for nomads), and 100 for the 28 directly elected seats in the Meshrano Jirgah. By no means all of these candidates were hand-picked nominees of the King and his administration. Many of the elections were quite heatedly contested, and one provincial governor at least (to judge from the interview I had shortly after the election with the governor of Kunduz) had considerable difficulty in keeping alive a warm interest without letting the contest come actually to the boil. On the other hand, the local election commissions did a considerable amount of preliminary screening to ensure that no 'subversive' characters – that is to say, those who might too dramatically oppose the administation's programme – were allowed either to stand as candidates or to vote. They could also exercise a similar veto after a candidate had been elected, though I am not aware that they actually did so. The candidates themselves were largely local influential landowners – generally, but not always, of the predominant ethnic group in the locality. Six women candidates put themselves up for election and women were entitled to vote. Four of the women were elected, as we have seen, but the number of women voters was disappointingly small – mainly because husbands and fathers in many cases expressly forbade their womenfolk to participate in this open public activity.

The election campaign gave encouraging evidence of the goverment's desire for genuine debate between candidates, although in the absence of parties this had to be on a largely personal basis. Newspapers printed the name and picture of every candidate free; candidates were able to purchase both advertising space and airtime on Radio Kabul (at about £12 a minute for a maximum of five minutes); and the radio station itself ran an extensive series of explanatory programmes on how the elections were to work and what they were all about. (TV did not come to Kabul until 1978.) Throughout the campaign, provincial governors and other prominent local officials spent much time explaining to voters what kind of people they ought to vote for, that is to say, they were soliciting support for candidates sympathetic to the administration. Yet there is no evidence of other direct pressures being brought to bear on the electorate to influence their voting. Clearly, a man had to be able to dip substantially into his own purse to finance a campaign, and this naturally tended to limit candidature to the wealthier sections of the community; but, apart from this practical consideration, the field was open to all comers who could satisfy the qualificatory provisions laid down in the constitution. Considerable pains were taken also with the conduct of the ballot iself, both to ensure its secrecy and its accuracy. Each candidate had a separate ballot box with his name, photograph and electoral symbol on it and into one of these, in the privacy of a screened booth, the voter dropped his ballot paper to indicate his choice.

Despite these efforts, however, the election remained largely confined to intellectuals and city dwellers, as one might expect for the first election among a generally illiterate population. Even in the cities the poll was not high — from 5% to 10% of those eligible to vote — and in the rural areas it was often as little as 2%. Thus the first elected deputies of the Shura could not reasonably be called representative of the people as a whole, though they certainly were representative of the politically aware and interested (or organizable), with the towns naturally returning the more radical and unusual members. Moreover, in assessing the poll in rural areas with a very low turn-out of voters, one has to appraise with caution the merits of the multi-ballot box mode of voting. This reservation is reinforced by the fact that the concept of the secret ballot is quite alien to the long established 'open' democracy of the village or tribal jirgah where every man may be heard and in voting must be seen to have the courage of his convictions. Many Afghans — whose ideal is to have as little contact with officialdom as possible — were suspicious that the ballot was just a device to identify them for taxation or conscription.

Yet the 1965 election can be seen as a clear, if limited success for the democratizers. There was virtually no indication of corruption or coercion; there was a competitive campaign and a fair ballot. The next step was to try to extend the interest in the electoral process through the municipal elections of 1966. But the poll was again low, as it was in the following general election of 1969. So what went wrong?

The division between legislature and executive was absolute: and it is perhaps in the way that this separation was organized that there lay the principal weakness of the 1964 constitution. The Prime Minister was appointed directly by the King and then recommended a list of ministers to him. Neither the Premier nor other ministers could be members of either house of parliament. The Premier then submitted his government to the Wolesi Jirgah for approval, first outlining its general policies to the lower house. The Wolesi Jirgah had the power to grant or withhold its vote of confidence, and it was the lower house alone that had this power of veto. (The all or nothing powers of the Wolesi Jirgah were not dissimilar to those of the European Parliament in its power to sack the whole EEC Commission but not an individual commissioner.) Only when the government received a vote of confidence could the King issue the necessary royal decree of appointment.

The Premier, however, had no machinery of party whips through which to exact that vote of confidence (the organized party as understood in the West being then still unknown in Afghanistan). The fall of the first government to hold power after the elections of October 1965 and its replacement by the next administration, demonstrated that the battle for ultimate power had yet to follow this preliminary skirmish between executive and legislature.

When Prince Daoud was forced in 1963 to resign the premiership, Dr Yusuf, an able but not very determined man, was appointed and held office as Premier for more than two years until the 1965 elections. With a PhD from Göttingen rather than influential family connections, Yusuf was the first meritocrat to reach the top in post-war Afghanistan.

When the new Shura met, he was again appointed Prime Minister by the King and with much the same cabinet as before, almost as if there had been no elections. But, surprisingly and encouragingly, the Wolesi Jirgah, raw as it was to the business of parliamentary democracy, showed its teeth, accused some of the members of the Yusuf government of bribery and corruption, and was only with the greatest difficulty persuaded to give its vote of confidence. Certain left-wing members led by Nur Mohammed Taraki, continued to protest and invited the students of Kabul University to come in a body to support their objection. The mass of the students were forcibly restrained from entering the parliamentary building; the inspirers of their demonstration urged them to force their way in on the following day on the grounds that it was their right to be present.* In the riots which ensued three people were killed, one a bystander, but the crackdown on legal outlets for student opinion that followed was to contribute significantly to the still more tragic demise of all party democracy. Many who were students then have carried their resentment into the towns and villages where they are teachers and officials now. This disturbance was largely instrumental in inducing Dr Yusuf to resign — in anguish of conscience, his supporters claimed, at the three deaths which occurred — and Muhammad

---

*An unquestionable breach of Art. 57, paragraph 3 of the constitution which stated that 'Nobody may enter the meeting place of the Shura by force.'

Maiwandwal was invited to form a government. But the tension between government and Shura was by no means over, although much less severe than before.

Maiwandwal submitted his government and its policy for approval, and comfortably got his vote of confidence. He then interpreted the constitution as permitting him to make individual changes in the composition of his cabinet without submitting them for approval to the Wolesi Jirgah. This interpretation he acted on, and insisted (as I found in conversation with him) that he was correct in so doing. Members of parliament thereupon exercised their right to question ministers and used it to criticize the Prime Minister for making these new appointments without first seeking the approval of the Wolesi Jirgah. However, since debate is not permitted on ministerial replies, they could do nothing more, short of moving a 'specific and direct' vote of no confidence in the government as a whole and this, in the country's unsettled state, they were reluctant to do for some time.

Maiwandwal, plagued with ill-health, resigned and Nur Ahmed Etemadi took office. In 1968, after much delay and fierce debate, the bill legalizing political parties – but not of course the non-Islamic, atheist, Communist Party – was passed by the Shura, but when the second election under the new constitution was called in 1969, the King had still not had the confidence to sign and so enact the bill. Fatally, therefore, the elections were contested only by independents. Though the 10%+ poll was a slight improvement on the 1965 election, it could scarcely be called a triumph for the democratic process. As independents, candidates were virtually all extremely conservative landowners or businessmen able to finance their own campaigns. Far more non-Pathans were elected but not a single woman, and almost three-quarters of the members of the Wolesi Jirgah were taking a parliamentary seat for the first time. The elections were slightly rigged in the sense that great influence was employed to ensure the defeat of such able opponents of the government as Farhang and Maiwandwal. Polling ouside the urban areas was negligible and the Marxist faction in the Wolesi Jirgah was reduced from five to three. Among the Leftists was a new member, a certain Mr Hafizullah Amin.

Amin, an American educated maths teacher, claimed that he had become a socialist as a result of his experiences in the United States. A man of ruthless ambition, brutality and administrative skills, but without any family connection with the essential power bloodlines of Afghanistan, I suspect that he saw the extra-parliamentary activities of the recently formed (but unofficial) People's Democratic Party as his best means of climbing from his lower middle-class origins to a position of power. He rapidly became a key member of the PDP and a staunch, though it later transpired expedient, supporter of Taraki. The PDP therefore continued to concentrate on extra-parliamentary activities amongst students and junior officers, both now going to Russia in increasing numbers for training. The arbitrary change of the entry conditions to Kabul University to favour applicants from the American school, and perhaps surreptitious pot-stirring by the Chinese, made the young a more fruitful, if still limited, source of recruitment for the Marxist groups.

The deadlock in parliament between the legislature and executive grew worse. In the 1969/70 session, for example, only one, very minor bill was passed.

A major reason for this situation was to be found in the composition of the Wolesi Jirgah. The standard of debate was poor, the quality of members in general, poorer.

There was an enormous contrast between the two or three dozen able members and the rest, the bulk of whom merely fulfilled the minimum requirements of sanity, literacy and attainment of their twenty-fifth birthday. For the most part they were small landowners, chosen for their local influence rather than for any wider ability or knowledge. Ultra-conservative in outlook they yet lacked any coherent philosophy of conservatism. They concentrated simply on resisting any proposal for taxing land or animals which might diminish their own wealth. It was not simply that the Shura's debates, if those I saw were anything to go by, were considerably more disorderly than those of the House of Commons, and its members inexperienced in the art of parliamentary discussion. More serious was the lack of any imaginative approach to the country's problems. Although legislators in many a western state can be just as unimaginative, in Afghanistan this deficiency is not made up by a strong outside body of political thinking or an informed public opinion capable of perceiving national needs and the policies necessary to meet them. The initiative lay almost exclusively with the government, apart from a handful of deputies with the ability to devise and present legislative proposals. The members of the Maiwandwal administration and the subsequent Etemadi, Zafir and Shafiq cabinets were, generally speaking, able men whose ideas were tempered with realism. The political weakness of the system lay in the absence of any real *collective* alternative other than that of the former Yusuf cabinet, which contained a number of able ministers relegated to impotent obscurity in the provinces. However unjustly to individuals, this alternative group carried a collective label of venality.

Corruption has always presented a major problem in

Afghan government whether under an absolute monarchy, a democratic monarchy, or a Marxist autocracy. In 1966, for example, an attempt was made to take what was a courageous initial step against the acceptance of corruption as a normal and inevitable ingredient in the Afghan way of life, by imprisoning a judge for taking bribes. The problem was to draw a dividing line between corruption and the customarily permissible nepotism – indeed, to know just how far it is practicable to go in the tight-knit society of the Afghan governing classes in breaking down that nepotism in favour of a meritocracy. A former Minister of the Interior once pointed out to me with tolerant cynicism that, within hours of a great set-to at question time in the Wolesi Jirgah, the very deputies who had denounced his supposed corruption would be round at his office to beg posts for their sons, cousins and nephews.

Such practices were bound to continue as long as the government remained the only considerable source of patronage and as long as parliamentary, ministerial and civil service salaries were so low that they made some form of supplementary income – by private enterprise in some instances, by taking bribes in many others – almost a matter of survival. Moreover, it was unreasonable to expect wholly 'clean' democratic government so long as there was no united opposition ready to replace the government at the first sign of failure. But with that perverse yet encouragingly characteristic Afghan independence of mind, the members of the Wolesi Jirgah were perfectly capable of banding together for the purpose of harassing the government. The weapon they chiefly used was the repeated demand that individual ministers answer questions on demand, not just on the rare occasion when the premier of the day put them up before the Wolesi Jirgah. In 1971 they brought down

Etemadi's government by a threat of a vote of no confidence on this issue. His successor, Dr Zafir, lasted a
bare year to December 1972 before falling before the
same threat, this time when famine afflicted much of
the north part of the country. Dr Shafiq's ensuing six
months in office were ended rather differently. It is
against such a background of confusion and frustration
in the offical machinery of democracy that the development of the underground Marxist parties in Afghanistan
has to be seen.

The People's Democratic Party of Afghanistan was
founded – unofficially of course – in 1965. Its structure
was strongly influenced by that of the Soviet Communist Party. Its two leading lights were Nur Mohammed Taraki and Babrak Karmal, a lawyer with a flair for
the dramatic. (Dupree recounts how, when injured in
hospital after a Wolesi Jirgah fight in 1966, he hastily
bound a few extra bandages round his head before coming the window to wave to his supporters.) Karmal was
elected to the Wolesi Jirgah in 1965 and my discussions
with him shortly afterwards indicated that while he was
a conventional Marxist idealogue – where Taraki was a
very impractical romantic revolutionary – he then envisaged an advance to socialism through the electoral
process under cover of the traditional United Democratic Front. This was an optimistic, or perhaps expedient view, considering that his parliamentary support
was no more than two or three members including the
woman member, Dr Anahita Ratebzad. Taraki, however, an intellectual and competent man of letters, was
generally regarded as the leader of the Afghan Left and
though his weekly magazine *Khalq* (the masses) only appeared for half-a-dozen editions before it was closed
down, it gave its name to the predominant group in the
PDP and indicated the staunchly nationalist and inde-

pendent line adopted by the majority of the Party. Karmal was much more an orthodox international Marxist toeing the Moscow line as required. These differences between the two leaders were eventually to lead to a split in the Party and just prior to the 1969 elections it was Karmal's *Parcham* (the flag) faction of the Party which was to produce the Party weekly of that name – as short-lived as its predecessor and closed before the polls opened. After the 1969 election, Amin, from his new position of influence in the Wolesi Jirgah, began to take over much of the role as Taraki's first lieutenant. The split between the two factions became open in 1973. Taraki refused to obey the Moscow directive to support the coup in which Daoud overthrew the monarchy and declared himself President, but Karmal moved himself and his Parchamis into the mainstream of power by doing so. Not until most of the Parchamis had been banished to the wilderness and it was clear that the orthodox Left would get nowhere as long as President Daoud ruled, did the two factions, under considerable pressure from Moscow, reunite to plot the Prince's overthrow. Both factions had tried hard to recruit in the 1960s and 1970s, not just among the intellectuals but in the army, air force, and police, into whose ranks they also infiltrated their own men. A key role in this strategy was played by Amin, though Parcham perhaps did a little better among those actually influenced while training abroad. It should be emphasized however, that very few of the ten thousand or so military personnel who had been trained abroad to that date were sympathetic, let alone recruited to the PDP. At the very height of its strength, just before the Daoud overthrow in 1978, it is doubtful whether the PDP ever had more than five or six thousand members all told.

But the Khalq and Parcham groups did not occupy the

most leftward position in Afghan politics in the late 1960s; that position was reserved for the group involved with another short-lived journal *Shu'la-yi-Jawed,* published by the brothers Mahmudi. This mounted verbal attacks indiscriminately against the Russians, the Americans, the irredentist nationalists, the mullahs and the royal family, though reserving its sharpest abuse and the vilest epithet – revisionist – for its political neighbours in the PDP.

Largely because political parties were not legal, a profusion of publications and associated unofficial groupings sprang up at the time of the 1965 elections. Many of the ablest of the deputies belonged to a group which centred round the shrewd, able and pleasant personality of Mohammed Siddiq Farhang, one of the deputies for Kabul, who gave up a ministerial appointment in order to take part in the genesis of politics in Afghanistan. When I questioned him about the formation of a political party, he laughingly told me that he was a very legalistically minded man and that, since parties were not yet legal, he had taken no steps to form one. Then, watching me with a twinkle, he added after a pause that, of course, he had sounded his fellow deputies' opinions on political subjects and discovered those who were like-minded. There seemed to be only about a dozen or fifteen of these 'like-minded' deputies (although, in contesting the office of Secretary of the Wolesi Jirgah, Farhang obtained a quarter of the total votes). The 'like-minded' might be encompassed by the term he used to indicate his own affiliation with international political elements: 'liberal democratic parties with social tendencies'. Certainly, he and his colleagues drew inspiration from the European social democrats, but more particularly from the progressive parties from such other underdeveloped countries as Burma, India and Egypt.

The basis of his economic policy was that the state must play a major role, almost an exclusive one, in the development of the backward economy of such an underdeveloped nation as Afghanistan, and that the consequence of the need for capital resources to achieve this development must be a policy of neutrality – a line not so far removed from that of Karmal.

The constitution certainly made provision for this type of policy to be exercised subject to certain limitations, and, paradoxically, it was at least partially carried out by a government most of whose individual members looked on Farhang himself as a dangerous radical. Farhang also appreciated what the fundamental nature of Afghan politics would be for the next decade – the politics of the intellectuals and not of the masses. He realized as clearly as his leftist rivals, that whoever could win the allegiance of the increasing numbers of technocrats who could not be fitted into the old nepotistic family patterns, would gradually establish political ascendancy.

Any political approach to the masses, other than perhaps one based on a simple and fanatical dressing up of Islam, could have little hope of success when the national literacy level was below 10%, communications were physically so difficult, and the radio, and to a considerable extent the press, was under government control.

The other informal groups in the Wolesi Jirgah were perhaps less aware of this crucial fact. The largest was a virtually religious party led by the Mojaddedis who now head one of the more religiously fanatical groups of freedom fighters. There was, in addition, a small economically conservative group committed to laissez-faire and private enterprise, a group whose principal objective was to create the wider Pathan empire envisaged in Pushtunistan, and a national party headed by Khalilullah Khalili, a poet and very much a King's man committed to seeing the constitution evolve on the lines envisaged by Zahir Shah. After he left office Maiwandwal also set up a highly personalized party (confusingly also known as the PDP) which pursued a line very similar to Khalili's.

Formal political debate on any large scale outside the Shura was made very difficult by a nervous administration. When *Khalq* appeared in April 1966, its editorial style was slightly hysterical and many of its articles (and the particular style of Tajiki Persian) seemed to show the influence of the banned Tudeh (Communist) Party in neighbouring Persia. This need not, however, have been a permanent defect and friends of free expression in the country were privately urging Taraki to make his journal more typically Afghan. The government did not give the paper the chance; after only five issues, it was closed down on the grounds that it violated the constitution, ostensibly in response to demands for its suppression by members of the Shura. No specific charges were made to justify this, but I was told by the head of the government news agency that its advocacy of public ownership and the abolition of private property was the specific aspect that was regarded as impugning the constitution. Also the government put a number of other small papers out of business by much more subtle methods, such as persuading the editor to resign (under the press laws, no newspaper could be published without an editor).

Of the thirty newspapers and journals listed by Dupree in 1973, two-thirds were banned for at least a time in the democratic decade, most of them for good and many within weeks of their first publication. Some, of course, collapsed under financial pressures in a country where commercial advertising is virtually unknown and the support of either the government or a wealthy individual is essential. The majority, however, were closed like *Khalq* because they had in some way offended the authorities.

The development of a western style democratic political system in the 60s was hampered by many factors, but to me three of them have clearly been crucial. When not even a substantial minority of the adult population could read, there could be no mass circulation press and therefore no popular political movement involving the mass of the people. But freedom of speech is the natural birthright of the Afghan. The pungently expressed views about any government which can be heard in the *chai khanas* are an indication that, when every Afghan can read and write, successive administrations will find themselves appraised with equal vigour on paper. During the 60s, however, party politics were confined to the few and those electors who could overcome their suspicion of the whole system were influenced more by the local power of candidates than by their doctrines.

The deputies who were elected, in the main proved themselves to be both inflexible and intemperate and the total separation of the elected element from the executive resulted in the absence of that process of mutual accommodation necessary to effective democratic government.

Finally the reflexive panic of the King and his family associates whenever they or the system they had devised came under fire, meant that no coherent, legitimate opposition could develop. The only alternatives to the appointed government were, therefore, anarchy or autocracy.

8 COUPS SANS SURPRISE

'I have acted to abolish a corrupt and effete government, a pseudo-democracy based on personal and class interests which has taken Afghanistan to the edge of an abyss.' The Afghan citizen tuning in to radio Kabul on 17 July 1973 would have learned with those words that the experiment in democracy was over and his country had returned to its more usual method of changing government. There would have been little else to tell him that Prince Daoud, the 'red premier' of the 1950s, had finally grown tired of political emasculation. Daoud's coup, involving only a few hundred key members of the army and air force and masterminded by the man who was to become Afghanistan's coup specialist, Colonel Abdul Qadir, Deputy Commander-in-Chief of the Air Force, had been virtually bloodless. Fewer than half a dozen people had died in the process. The King was 'conveniently' out of the country. In view of the speed with which members of his family and entourage were released from captivity and sent to join him in Italy, it is hard to escape the suspicion that Zahir Shah, always more interested in sport and archaeology than government, had done a deal with his ambitious uncle.

It is hard, too, not to share Daoud's frustration and his strictures on the pseudo-democracy he swept aside. Deprived of the legitimate development of political parties and of a free press, it never had a chance. It was

more surprising perhaps, that an aristocrat of the old ruling clan and not one of the Marxist parties had staged
the coup. The fact is, however, that the latter were still
far too weak to act and wisely bided their time. They
were, too, in some disarray among themselves, and had
already divided into the Khalq and Parcham factions
whose relationship we shall examine in greater detail
later. Moscow had decreed that the PDP should support
Daoud, but Taraki's majority Khalq group had declined
to do so. Karmal's Parchami faction, however, toed the
party line both from conviction and expediency. Daoud
soon received further Soviet endorsement in the shape
of a state visit from President Podgorny.

Following the classic pattern, Daoud had within two
months 'discovered' a counterplot and imprisoned its
leaders, that is to say his critics. One of them, former
Premier Maiwandwal, was supposed to have hanged
himself in his cell.

Inevitably, Pakistan was accused of involvement in
the counter-revolution, as indeed it was again in the
following summer of 1974 when a further unsuccessful
attempt was made to overthrow Daoud. Pakistan firmly
rejected all such accusations, Bhutto's government trying to keep a delicate balance between the needs of
stability on its north-western border and the loyalty of
the Pathan tribes on its side of the same frontier.

At the outset of the five years of his second rule,
Daoud firmly surpressed any dissident Islamic groups
such as the Muslim League, which objected to the
degree of his involvement with the Soviet Union. With
Russian economic backing, he was able, in the early
years at least, to improve the Afghan economy and even
achieve a small balance of payments surplus. But like
virtually every other Afghan ruler in similar circumstances, he found it increasingly necessary, psycho-

logically and politically, to assert his independence of his patrons. In 1975 he began to purge the Marxists from the army and subtly diminish their political influence by despatching the enthusiastic young *aparatchiki*, the Parchamis,* to spread the socialist word in remote tribal wildernesses where he well knew it would fall on stony ground. He is reputed to have engineered the assassination of half a dozen prominent Leftists and was certainly exiling even his moderate critics. He began, also, to repair his relations with religious leaders. By 1977 he had not only begun to modify his hard line on the Pushtunistan question and to arrange an exchange of state visits to Pakistan, but had promised new legislative elections in 1979 which would inevitably have brought substantial conservative elements back into the political arena. This antagonized the members of the People's Democratic Party whom he had used as the political basis of his own team at the time of the coup. In 1978 Daoud began purging again, still more drastically, and when he openly expressed the view that Cuba, Russia's proxy in Africa, should be expelled from the non-aligned nations group for its interference in that continent, his days were numbered. Daoud's Marxism was expedient rather than ideological. He used it and the Soviet and PDP support that were its corollary, as a means to obtain and hold power in pursuit of purely Afghan objectives, an approach which neither Moscow nor its loyal Afghan disciples could allow to prevail for long.

His opponents initiated their counter-measures in November 1977 when they assassinated his close associate Ali Ahmed Khoram, the Minister of Planning. The inevitable 'trial' followed against a background of

---

*Again we must remember that we are thinking in terms of very small numbers only – in this case some one hundred and fifty men.

food shortages and student unrest. The accused did not yet include the key political and military figures who were Daoud's real enemies, amongst and against whom he did not yet feel secure enough to move openly. Nevertheless, no suitable pretext for his overthrow immediately offered itself to this opposition group. However, on 17 April 1978 Mir Akbar Khaiber, a former leader of Parcham, was assassinated — by whom it was not clear, though the KGB, with a 'team' now in Afghanistan, came under some suspicion and was undeniably involved in helping to engineer the subsequent coup. The funeral on 19 April turned into a large-scale anti-American demonstration which gave Daoud the excuse he needed to arrest the PDP ruling triumvirate of Taraki, Amin and Karmal a week later. However, he made the mistake of leaving a number of his other former 1973 fellow conspirators at large, including Mr Coup himself, Colonel Abdul Qadir. On 28 April the Colonel struck again, using carefully selected units of the army and air force headed by Soviet trained officers who were either members of PDP or sympathetic to it.

This time the coup was far from bloodless. Tanks and MiG 21s attacked the presidential palace, army headquarters and other key points. At many of them, for Daoud had a strong personal following in the armed forces, the revolutionaries were resisted. Daoud himself was shot down in cold blood, but not before he had seen more than a score of his family and close supporters butchered before his eyes. In the land of the blood feud it is always considered safer to kill possible avengers pre-emptively while you are at the business of murder.

By the end of the month, the PDP trio had been released and the new Democratic Republic of Afghanistan (in Newspeak) had been established under a Revolutionary Council whose chairman was Nur Muhammed Taraki, who also became Premier. The two other PDP leaders, Amin and Karmal, both became Deputy Premiers. At this stage the Council still contained some influential former supporters of Daoud, such as Aslam Watanyar, who was, however, moved away from the key Portfolio of Defence to the relatively harmless one of Communications.

Taraki probably owed his emergence as leader of the new régime more to his reputation for being independent of the Soviet line than to his personality. I had found him likeable to talk to but clearly, even in the 60s, a man of ideas rather than action. It was important to the newcomers to try to prevent tribal resistance to the first purely Marxist, non-dynastic government of Afghanistan both by paying lip-service to the pre-eminence of Islam in the philosophy of government, and by denying that their coup was communist or Soviet inspired. Much evasive language was employed on Kabul radio, especially by Colonel Qadir, who acknowledged that while the revolution was Marxist in a popular sense, there was no Communist Party as such in Afghanistan and that the new leaders were all good Muslims. Nevertheless, between May and July, some twenty-five trade agreements were signed with the Soviet Union and others with Eastern Bloc countries. Particularly important were those for the additional exploitation of oil and gas and for the building of a linking road and rail bridge and associated communication system across the Oxus at Hayratan. It soon became clear that the Afghan economy could function only by grace of Russian aid. Taraki sought to popularize his government by cancelling all debts and mortgages to money lenders and promising to limit land holdings to fifteen acres and to distribute the surplus of the feudal landowners, about

80% of Afghanistan's agricultural land, to poor peasants. He also planned to abolish the traditional bride price and launch a national literacy campaign aimed equally at both sexes – all these measures would have seriously undermined the privileges of the exclusively male, conservative and primitively Muslim leaders of the rural communities. It was also his intention, in his own words, 'to nationalize anything that is worth nationalizing.'

At the outset of Taraki's régime all the provincial governors, even in the non-tribal areas, had been replaced by military commanders but tribal unrest continued to increase throughout the summer of 1978 and was not even checked by Taraki's resumption of an irredentist line over Pushtunistan. It also soon emerged that several thousand people had been killed and some five thousand imprisoned during the coup rather than the 'not more than seventy-two or seventy-three' that Taraki had been claiming. Strong man of the new triumvirate was undoubtedly Amin, who was soon drastically to step up the volume of execution and imprisonment. Although some thousand PDP prisoners were released, by the end of May non–PDP politicians, including anyone who had been a minister during the previous twenty years, senior officers of the armed forces, civil servants and merchants had been arrested and imprisoned in considerable numbers. It was Amin's influence too, which in July secured the dismissal of Parcham group leaders Babrak Karmal and Nur Muhammed Nur (the Interior Minister), and their despatch to embassies abroad, while he had himself made Party Secretary of the PDP. Early in August Karmal attempted to return from Moscow, but was arrested after a gunfight at Kabul airport and again despatched abroad. It is hard to see why he was not executed but the logic of Afghan acts of mercy is often as inexplicable as some of their wanton killings, a certain whimsical arbitrariness has pervaded Afghan power struggles throughout the country's history. A few days later yet another plot was discovered and several men who had been instrumental in the overthrow of Daoud, were themselves arrested, including Abdul Qadir.

Afghanistan's economic survival was by now firmly dependent on the patronage of the Soviet Union. Its Russian paymasters suggested to a more than willing Taraki that he insure his régime against counter-revolution by entering, in December 1978, into the kind of defence treaty which had enabled the Soviet Union to secure unpopular régimes by military force elsewhere.

Early in February 1979 newly arrived American ambassador Dubs, was kidnapped by a 'bandit gang' in Kabul and shot, possibly by the Russians involved in the subsequent rescue. Dubs has been alleged to have been a specialist in subversion and insurgency and although there is absolutely no proof of his involvement at this stage, the rest of the year was certainly to see a dramatic growth in the scale and scope of revolt against the Taraki régime and its open dependence on the Soviet Union. As soon as spring broke the paralysis of the Afghan winter, there was, on 12 March, a major uprising in Herat in which several hundred PDP members and their families and sympathizers were killed. A number of those killed and reportedly flayed alive were Soviet advisers, and it was not long before a top level military team under General Alexei Yepishev, First Deputy Minister of Defence and General Secretary of Political Affairs for the Russian Army and Navy, arrived on a 'tour of inspection'. General Yepishev had played a major role in the 1968 Russian invasion of Czechoslovakia. There was, moreover, a considerable build up in the influx of Soviet military hardware, though the equipment (MiG 21 fighters and Mi24 helicopter gunships and T62 tanks) was by no means the most modern available. Estimates of the numbers killed in the retaliatory action to restore government control in Herat varied between one thousand and five thousand. Between May and September there were ever more frequent and substantial desertions from the Afghan army and increasingly successful and savage attacks by guerrillas on convoys and military and administrative posts. Again Soviet advisers were numbered amongst those killed. In March Amin had replaced Taraki as Prime Minister, but Taraki remained titular Head of State. There were only four new ministers in Amin's first cabinet and though Taraki relinquished the Defence Portfolio, it went to his loyal supporter Colonel Watanyar while the Interior Ministry was put into the hands of another Taraki man.

Amin was now effectively running the Afghan government and his response to the combination of growing insurgency and the diminishing reliability of the Afghan army was to try to establish a military arm of the PDP, to be known as khalqis, and 'people's courts' to mete out instant 'justice' to 'counter-revolutionaries', among whom members of the Parcham wing of PDP were to be numbered. In July, Amin took over executive responsibility for defence, though Taraki remained nominally responsible and Commander-in-Chief of the Armed Forces. At the same time Colonel Watanyar was demoted from Defence to the still important Interior Ministry, and the Interior Minister was moved to Border Affairs.

More disturbing was the ferocity of Amin's punitive raids on recalcitrant villages. It is clear not only from Karmal's subsequent denunciatory catalogue of his crimes, but from numerous rebel sources that children were being tortured and butchered before their parents' eyes, villages were razed to the ground and their entire populations either massacred or forcibly moved to other parts of the country.

In an unconvincing attempt to explain the total inability of the government to control many areas in a country which it claimed to be '98% behind the revolution' the state-controlled media put out a steady spate of accusations of 'foreign intervention by Iranian and Pakistani imperialists sending troops disguised as civilians into Afghanistan.' The United States and China were inevitably bracketed in these accusations, though publicly, at least, America had so far done no more than stress through one or two influential senators and at the UN that outside intervention in the troubled affairs of Afghanistan should at all costs be avoided. The governments of Iran and Pakistan repeatedly denied that they played any role, other than as humanitarian hosts to refugees, in the insurgency within Afghanistan. International reaction was succinctly summed up by the Indian Prime Minister, Morarji Desai, – so very different from Mrs Gandhi's view – when he told President Brezhnev that 'the Kabul government should try to acquire credibility among the Afghan people instead of blaming Pakistani interference for its troubles.'

It is not easy to be clear about the events which led to Amin's dispensing with the umbrella of Taraki's reputation and replacing him as Head of State. Taraki made a visit to Moscow in September on which his sponsors expressed their disquiet at the imminent prospect of a successful right wing counter-revolution if Amin's brutalities were not halted. Such a view accorded with Taraki's own repugnance at the retributive policies of his powerful Prime Minister, but that same squeamishness led him to forgo the usual Afghan argument of a bullet in the brain and try persuasion. Amin was quick to see what was in the wind and while Watanyar was trying to organize the arrest of the Prime Minister, Amin counterordered his arrest and that of the Border Affairs Minister and others who fled to the hills only just in time to save their lives.

On the same day it appears that the Russian Ambassador had invited Amin and Taraki to a meeting, ostensibly to discuss the current situation but in practice, it seems more likely, to neutralize Amin. In the ensuing shoot-out, however, it was Taraki who was fatally wounded, though Radio Kabul kept up the pretence that he was alive for some two weeks and then suggested that he had died from natural causes. Taraki's pictures vanished from public places within days of the shooting incident, and as early as 17 September, Moscow cut its losses and endorsed the new incumbent in a congratulatory telegram. The following week Russian combat troops entered Afghanistan in strength for the first time. The three battalions involved were probably largely made up of the specialist troops used to make ready the way for more substantial forces – as they had in Czechoslovakia. It is difficult to believe that this was done without the consent of Amin, if not by his direct invitation. During the same week Amin made sweeping cabinet changes to bring in his own men, including his brother as Chief of Intelligence, and dismissed the governors of a number of provinces. He was faced, however, with the virtually insoluble problem presented by the fact that even at the height of its success the PDP probably had no more than five to six thousand members, a figure drastically reduced by the internecine quarrels of the previous eighteen months. Outsiders would clearly have to be brought in and there would be few of these to be found in Afghanistan itself. The Afghan armed services were already threaded through with an extensive network of Soviet advisers, even down to company level. In order to ensure loyalty Amin had no option but to further extend this network.

Amin's régime was short-lived and expired in as thick

a cloud of mystery as that in which it was born. Though rebel claims to control half the country's twenty-six provinces were certainly exaggerated, there were unarguably major 'no-go' areas for the government. By tacit admission Badakshan in the north-east was virtually in Tajik and Pathan hands, as was the Hazarajat, Nuristan and large parts of the provinces of Paktya and Kunar. Incidents such as that in which an Afghan army unit sent to attack Hazara rebels in Wardak simply handed over its weapons to them, made certain control beyond the capital virtually impossible. Against this deteriorating background it seems to me perfectly plausible that Amin *did* ask for Soviet military help. How else can one explain the fact that he did not publicly object to the arrival of Soviet airborne troops on 17 December – a good week before he fell from power. After all, such an objection, if they had been present against his will, would have been politically expedient in demonstrating his independence of Russia to the tribesmen, and diplomatically expedient in enlisting world opinion to forestall the more massive Soviet intervention which followed. It seems more likely that following the invasion he was killed by accident when his bodyguard started fighting the 'protective' encircling Russians in a paranoid reflex, or that he was simply double-crossed. In view of his response to Taraki's suggestion that he step aside, he may well have reacted violently to the proposal that he quietly make way for the very men he had banished – Panshiri and Karmal – and been killed by the Russian troops of General Viktor Paputin, the Soviet general in charge of the coup. The embarrassment caused by the elimination of the one man who could 'legitimize' their invasion would have infuriated the Russian leadership, already frustrated at the major failure in their foreign policy implicit in the necessity to intervene militarily in Afghanistan. The best was made of a bad job on 27

December by announcing that Amin had been 'executed' in the hope that this would win Karmal some support among those who had been outraged by Amin's atrocities. The anticipated anger of the Politburo could certainly account for General Paputin's suicide. But speculation, though it may be fun, is quite irrelevant, since it had long been apparent that without the Soviet prop, any left wing reformist government in Kabul must fall in the face of reaction. So thin are the remaining ranks of indigenous Marxists that there are scarcely any members of the PDP in Karmal's government.

The pattern of the Soviet invasion is interesting. Once the key airfields of Begram and Kabul had been secured by the advance units in late autumn, the invasion was spearheaded by the elite of the Soviet armed forces – the Airborne Divisions. These seven divisions (a division = three regiments of three battalions each containing about four to five hundred men) are the best trained, best paid and best equipped in the USSR. Indeed it was their equipment, the ASU 85 armoured infantry fighting vehicle and the new AKS 74 automatic rifle, which betrayed the identity of these early troops. The Airborne Divisions (the 4th and 105th were probably involved, though regiments from others may have been included to 'blood' a good cross section) do not come under any army command but answer directly to the Politburo. Quite a large proportion even of the other ranks are regulars (in contrast to the rest of the army in which they are virtually all conscripts) and members of the Communist Party or Komsomol, thus suiting them to politically sensitive tasks. They are also almost all Greater (i.e. European) Russians unlike other units of the Russian army where, right down to company level, the races are deliberately mixed. The back-up troops, numbering some eighty thousand by the beginning of

March 1980, were probably of this mixed nature, though such is the flexibility of the Soviet army that there may have been an initial preponderance of troops from the Asiatic republics — many of whom were reported to have been replaced by non-Asian troops in March.

The main army invaded almost entirely through the long prepared Kushka/Herat highway and through the Oxus ports of Termez and Sher Khan Banda and down the Kunduz/Kabul road. The Russian advisers were able to neutralize many of the units to which they were attached and for the first time an Afghan coup was carried out entirely by Russian troops. Unpopular as Amin was, no Afghan unit could be counted on to participate in what was virtually a foreign invasion. By the end of December, while the West still digested its turkey and Christmas pudding, the Russians had occupied all the key towns, airfields and highways before the winter snows had restricted movement — and thus reduced guerrilla actions to bands of small number. Russian troops kept a low profile and were seldom engaged in direct combat with Afghans except in dealing with rebellious units of the Afghan army or when Afghan troops faced certain defeat, as they did at Faizabad in January. Soviet piloted helicopter gunships and MiG 21s had, on the other hand, carried out many strikes, though the majority of air attacks had been flown by Soviet trained Afghan pilots. Until the summer of 1980 Russian forces could have disengaged relatively easily and quickly. Now, without some accomodation with the freedom fighters, such a withdrawal would be fraught with military hazard. The brutal, ruthless and indiscriminate campaign waged ever more directly by the Russians, not only against the guerrillas but also against the civilian population in their areas of operation, has built up a legacy of revenge which will not easily be redeemed. The total collapse of morale in the Afghan army, to the point where its effective strength is no more than a fifth of the 1979 level, means that a phased withdrawal and transfer of power to Afghan forces has become impractical. So what happens now?

9 MATE?

Lord Curzon, not renowned for his modesty, once remarked that 'no man who has ever read a page of Indian history will every prophesy about the frontier.' All one can sensibly offer at this time is an appraisal of the conflicting forces in that area and some analysis of the problems facing the West over Afghanistan.

A necessary starting point is the recognition that the Soviet invasion of Afghanistan (in 1980 at least) was a failure, not a triumph of Russian foreign policy and is seen as such in the Kremlin. Afghanistan was by then on the brink of a successful and highly reactionary counter-revolution and nothing that lay within the Kabul régime's unaided power could have halted it. The Soviet Union was faced with the choice of seeing most of the work and treasure of the past two decades wasted, or coming to the military assistance of its protégé. It chose the latter course as the lesser evil. But can even Russian military might prop up the Karmal régime? If it does, what can, and does, such a régime hope to achieve? How effective are the forces ranged against the Afghan government and its Russian allies? Have they any prospect of success and what kind of Afghanistan do they seek? If there is a protracted stalemate what will be the consequences to Afghanistan, its neighbours, or, indeed, the world at large?

Only to pose such questions is to highlight the uncertainties and the dilemma of western governments trying to determine the line they should take. It is probably easiest to begin with an assessment of the position of the freedom fighters.

The Pathan groups fall into two main categories; those which belong to the Teiman Atahad Islami and those which do not. The first attempt at formal co-operation between rebel groups came in March 1979, with the formation of a national liberation front led by Imam Seghbatullah Mojaddedi, one of the Mojaddedi family which had played such a significantly conservative role by virtue of its religious authority during the democratic period. The two other main component groups of the front were Burhanuddin Rabbani's Jamaat-i-Islami, which drew very heavily for its leadership and support on the Pakistan National Alliance which had provided most of the civilian element in President Zia's first government, and Maulavi Mohammadi's Movement for the Islamic Revolution. The fourth component was a faction of the Hizb-i-Islami, the Islamic Party, under Mohammad Yunus Khales.

It is significant that Seghbatullah Mojaddedi was found the most acceptable leader of the original freedom fighters front, for he was undoubtedly a fanatical, and, in western liberal terms, reactionary religious fundamentalist, who if in power would be more likely to restore the rigours of purdah than to accelerate the emancipation of women, to tighten the grasp of the mullahs on education and land rather than to indulge in land reforms or mount a mass literacy campaign. To a much lesser extent the same is true of the urbane and sophisticated Gailani who despite the name of his group would like to see a basically theocratic state. Both of these leaders have been accused by a communist press in Afghanistan and in Russia, which seems to get rather muddled in its time scale, of being British agents. The freedom that these and other Pathan guerrilla leaders seek is essentially freedom from foreign interference rather than freedom in the western sense. They seek freedom not just physically but intellectually, the freedom to carry on in the old ways and some groups even go so far as to seek to restore the monarchy.

There were a number of very significant omissions from the front. The main body of Hizb led by its founder Gulbaddin Hekmatyar did not join. Nor did the Harekat Islami Afghanistan led by Sheikh Mohammed Assef Mohseni. This group is based in Iran – the largest of the sixty-odd groups which I was told operated from there. Mohseni made a number of impassioned broadcasts from Teheran denouncing the Soviet invasion and had the open support of the Ayatollah Shariatamadri. The really important absentee, however, was the leader of probably the most effective Pathan freedom fighter group based outside the country – Sayed Ahmed Gailani. The group goes by the somewhat long-winded name of the Afghan Islamic and Nationalistic Revolution Council. In August 1979 Gailani, together with some lesser independents, decided to join the national front groups to set up the Teiman, with its headquarters in Peshawar, to attempt to both co-ordinate military activities within Afghanistan and, in many respects more importantly, the appeal to outside governments and individuals for military and financial support.

Yet to date they have been singularly unsuccessful. The Muslim world as with one voice fiercely denounced the Russian invasion, yet has been conspicuously reluctant to fund the rebels; Pakistan has accepted almost a million refugees and given asylum to guerrilla leaders, yet it restricts the extent to which those leaders can train their men and mount their operations from Pakistan's soil; while some Iranian leaders have openly backed the freedom fighters, official pronouncements have contained only muted criticism, if any; the West passes resolutions and encouragement but little more; China produces unlimited criticism of the Soviet Union and very limited supplies of arms. In short, the freedom fighters, while having the sympathy of three-quarters of a nervous world, in practice stand alone.

Another problem is that of finding a leader of sufficient character and charisma to be acceptable to all the rebels − or even all the Pathans. The Afghans *can* unite under the leadership of a truly great man, who fulfils the image described and exemplified by Khushal Khan Khattaq but they are once-in-a-century figures and there is no sign of one now. Candidates as far as the Pathan groups are concerned, range from the slightly absurd suggestion of a 'restoration' of Amanullah's son Hassan Durrani, now a parfumier in New York, to a much more plausible figurehead, the once formidable General Aref, now in exile in Rome, or General Abdul Mustaghani, now in West Germany. However, the fact is that mutual suspicion comes much more naturally to the Pathans than mutual admiration and though family, village, clan and tribal loyalties are very important to them so is their absolute, almost anarchic, love of personal independence. Not for nothing does the Pushtu word for enmity (*turburgalay*) derive from the word for cousin (*turbur*).

Liaison between rebel leaders in New York, London and Peshawar and their adherents based in Afghanistan is naturally difficult and encourages the innate tendency of each band leader to act independently. It is clear to me from conversations with some of the internationally based leaders that they are very concerned for the morale of the men doing the fighting. They fear that while the guerrillas may not exactly lose heart, they will become bored and disillusioned at the lack both of major success and of outside support and therefore return to their normal pastoral and agricultural occupations, taking up arms against the Russians only now and then as the mood takes them. For this reason the leaders in exile were concentrating their efforts at the time of writing on setting up a mobile transmitter system in Pakistan from which they could broadcast encouragement to their own men and preach sedition and disaffection to the Afghan regulars opposing them and the Asiatic troops in the Russian army. But such a radio station could only improve communication with the Pathan groups operating south of the Hindu Kush and there are many Pathans of the diaspora fighting in the north of the country. The most spectacularly successful of these has been Haji Meheidin, a rough and ready man very different from the sophisticated intellectuals and religious leaders who head the Pakistan based groups. Together with the Tajik freedom fighters operating independently in the same province he had virtually removed Badakshan from Russian and Afghan army control by the spring of 1980. Indeed the Russians had to mount one of their biggest operations to save the government forces in Faizabad from being totally destroyed. Yet the Tajiks and the Pathans in this region have only the most rudimentary liaison. In fact the Tajik group, the Setem-i-Melli, was founded by its three leaders, Taher Badakshi, Vasef Bakhtali and Baruddin Bahes (two of whom were last reported in prison) as a political movement to resist Pathan domination. Other centres of non-Pathan resistance are, as might be expected, in the Hazarajat where ex-MP Wali Beg leads a force of some five thousand Hazara fighting men, the Hedadia Mujaheddin Islam Afghani. These at least have links with Mohseni's

Pathan group in Iran and arms from sympathetic Pathan units in the Afghan regular army.

In Nuristan, where rebellion against the Russian backed Taraki régime and its successors began, resistance is both fierce and fiercely and brutally repressed. Here Khalilu Nuristani leads a group of guerrillas probably some three or four thousand strong who have received clothes, money and moral support from Gailani's group.

In Baluchistan Mir Chaus Bux Bizenjo, chief of one of the three main Baluch tribes, actively encourages his clansmen on the Afghan side of the border. The scene is further confused by various freelance groups of rebels operating throughout Afghanistan.

It is virtually impossible to gauge the effectiveness of the Afghan freedom fighters because the Afghans must rival the Welsh for the role of the world's greatest self-deceiving story tellers. If all rebel claims were added up the Russian army would have been wiped out several times over. This is in their classic tradition. A typical example is a village tale of Bachha-i-Saqao, the brigand who seized the throne for a few weeks in 1929 and who was eventually defeated by Nadir Shah.

'A traitorous general told Nadir Khan about an unguarded path to Kabul. Shah Wali took a force to Kabul and found Bachha-i-Saqao in the Bala (fort) with only four hundred men. Forty thousand of the army of Shah Wali surrounded the Bacha who came forth alone with machine guns and drove off the entire force. . . .'[1] There is nothing new in the Afghan proclivity for exaggerating military success!

But reliable intelligence reports suggest Russian casualties in excess of three thousand by the end of March 1980 and eyewitness accounts, such as that of Barrie Penrose who travelled much of the main communications network early in April 1980, at least report evidence of burnt out tanks, troop transports and helicopters. The fact that photographs of Russian tanks show mine-sweeping attachments suggests that Soviet troops are having to work at keeping the roads clear and the fact that tanks have been captured when the Russians had ample fire power and recovery vehicles to ensure, if sufficiently determined, that knocked-out tanks do not fall into the hands of lightly armed rebels, suggests that morale may not always be very high. The Peshawar based resistance movements in fact claim active defections from the Soviet ranks but they cannot produce any defectors. Other sources suggest to me that disaffection rather than defection is the consequence in the non-crack Russian units of being called on to fight a population which they had been told would welcome them as liberators. The rebel excuse that taking prisoners is inconvenient does not really ring true (though the erroneous belief that Afghans do not take prisoners, or probably torture them to death, may partially account for the refusal of Russian troops to defect or surrender).

Commentators are sometimes tempted to draw parallels between Afghanistan and Vietnam, but the very different circumstances of the anti-government forces is only one of the many ways in which that analogy is false. The Afghans do not have the direct military support of a contiguous major power, they do not have a base territory under their own control from which to operate, they do not have the support of a peace movement in their enemy's home country, above all, they do not have the unity of either purpose or belief enjoyed by the Viet Cong.

This last assertion may seem strange in view of the frequent claims made by rebel leaders that they are conducting a *Jihad*, a holy war, against the Russian invaders. Certainly the fact that the Russians subscribe to an atheist view of life totally repugnant to the Muslim Afghans is used as a means of inciting groups of rebels on a local and immediate basis to wage war on the invaders, but the western assumption that the defence of Islam in the face of the ungodly is the prime motivating force for the ordinary Mujaheddin is wrong. As an Afghan commentator put it in 1951, in the context of the Pushtunistan dispute, 'thus the real source of the uprising in the Pakhtun territory lay in the passionate desire of the inhabitants for the independence of their fatherland. Since the British belonged to a different faith, they habitually interpreted any opposition as arising from the religious sentiment of the people and ignored their impatience for independence from all foreign influence.'

It needs also to be remembered that in September 1978, long before the Russian invasion, the Taraki régime also declared a *Jihad* – against the rebels!

There is, then, some spasmodic co-operation between various groups but the general pattern is one of a large number of independent guerrilla leaders conducting their feudal, warlord-style campaigns. The Pathans are divided into two main factions and many lesser ones and the attitude of the non-Pathan rebels to the Pathans is usually best summed up in the old Tajik proverb 'trust a snake before a harlot and a harlot before a Pathan.' There is no doubt of the widespread loathing of the Russians and the determination of the vast majority of the (male) population to resist the invaders at all costs. The absence of any unified command however, not only greatly diminishes the rebels' military impact but means that there is no one with whom the Russians or their puppet government can negotiate peace. (Another point where the Vietnam parallel falls.)

The reluctance of Afghanistan's immediate neighbours to become deeply involved is not hard to understand. Iran is rent by internal conflict to the point where government has largely broken down and the once prosperous economy has collapsed. The adherents of the Ayatollahs Khomeini and Shariatamadri struggle for power; the Kurds in the north-west and the Baluch in the south-east are only the two most significant of the racial sub-groups striving for regional autonomy or independence; politicians and politically active students vie for power; the armed forces are in disarray and much demoralized; and the Tudeh party lurks forbidden in the shadows, well-organized and well-armed, waiting for the opportunity to impose Marxist rule on the country. All but this latter group know that to provoke the Soviet Union to the point where it felt able to make a 'legitimate' military intervention at the 'invitation' of its acolytes would spell the end of their ambitions. The greatest tragedy of the American attempt to rescue the Teheran hostages by military means was not its failure, or even the death of some of those involved, sad indeed as these were, but the fact that it had set a precedent for the one course of action which the West would find disastrous in this region. It is not now impossible that the western powers will find themselves faced with a choice either of accepting a crippling blow to their economies by the diversion of Iranian oil to the Soviet bloc or of an even more disastrous war. The economic sanctions proposed by President Carter, by driving the Iranians as surely through the door of the Russian pawnshop as the Afghans were driven, would simply achieve the same results over a longer time scale.

It is thus not surprising that while some disapproving noises are made by Iranian leaders, refugees are sheltered and a blind eye turned on the activities of the freedom fighters, the degree of help which Iran could give – particularly in weapons and training – is not forthcoming.

In Pakistan General Zia holds on to power only with great difficulty. He has allowed in large numbers of refugees on humanitarian grounds. Estimates vary greatly, but by the summer of 1980 they seem to number between three-quarters of a million and a million. How many of these are nomads who will recross the border in their traditional seasonal migrations cannot be estimated, nor can a figure easily be put on that propor-tion of the refugees who are in fact undercover guerrillas. If the Israelis can attack PLO refugee camps in other countries, on the grounds that they harbour terrorists, so can the Afghans or the Russians. Although General Zia has given asylum to Pathan rebel leaders and has tacitly condoned their campaigning and co-ordinating in Pesh-awar, he has repeatedly denied that he either encour-ages or allows training or armed attacks on Afghanistan to be based in Pakistan – which is not to say that he can prevent them or tries very hard in practice to do so. His second most important political consideration is to pre-vent at all costs a trans-border intervention in the other direction, in which Russian backed Pathans or Baluch are assisting the separatists on his side of the border (who are as yet still only a relatively small minority) to break away from the central government. While he could, perhaps surprisingly, probably rely on the loyalty of the locally recruited forces in resisting such incur-sions, the Punjabi units he might be called on to use as reinforcements would not only have little heart for the role but, if past experience is anything to go by, might be almost as unwelcome as the foreign invaders.

More significantly from Zia's point of view, if the

armed forces — among whose leaders there is already fierce criticism of his rule — were tied down on the frontier they could not be employed to maintain order throughout the rest of the country and his hold on power would weaken. His possible successors, the Bhuttos, have already criticized such support as he has given the Afghan rebels and scorned his fears of a Russian follow-up invasion as panic or self-preservation. They would abandon his relatively hard line and try to preserve the security of their frontiers by appeasement — not a conspicuously successful policy in dealing with the Russians. Zia has now declined to turn to the Americans for help, sensing in such a move further unpopularity, though his refusal is a cause of contention with his fellow generals. Yet while he probably could, with a reasonable degree of popular backing, fend off a second-hand invasion by Pathans or Afghan forces, he could not conceivably resist on his own the directly applied might of the Soviet Union for more than a few days. Would Afghanistan's other neighbour then come to his aid?

Though China has only a few miles of common border with Afghanistan, and that high in the almost inaccessible mountains of the Pamir, it does have a considerable interest in the outcome of the present struggle. China's alliance with Pakistan is the linchpin of its policy in the subcontinent, developed originally as a counterpoise to India and now significant in its struggle for the leadership of the communist world and in its defence strategy against Russia. The alliance is very practically symbolized by the great Karokoram highway. This considerable engineering feat in building the world's highest major road of such length was completed in 1978 and provides a direct link between China and Pakistan. A substantial increase in military traffic on it early in

1980 was indicative of China's concern to bolster Pakistan against the possibility of direct attack. The terms of their alliance are such that it is arguable that China would be bound in theory to come to Pakistan's aid if there were a Soviet invasion – though whether or not she did so would no doubt be determined by expediency.

A Chinese presence in Pakistan might well deter the Russians but would do nothing to improve Zia's domestic standing and might well prove as unwelcome in the long run as did that of Hengest and Horsa to the British king who sought their aid against the Picts. Yet there is no other practical way at present of bringing great power counter-pressure to Russia's 'southward advance in fulfilment of her historic destiny.' The issue is further complicated by the fact that it is to China's advantage that Russia should be heavily and lengthily embroiled in Afghanistan. China is supplying some arms to the Afghan freedom fighters to achieve this and guerrilla success in Badakshan, in particular, may not be unconnected with that province's proximity to China.

Such hawkish views are even more openly observable in the USA where commentators have gloatingly – and quite mistakenly as we have seen above – talked of Afghanistan as Russia's Vietnam. America has denied helping the Afghan freedom fighters and such American weapons as are being used by them may well have come from other sources. However, there is a school of thought both in the CIA and the administration which believes that the only thing that will check Russia's worldwide neo-colonial ambitions is burned fingers and that Afghanistan is the best opportunity yet to light the fire. So far the American government has resisted the temptation to stoke the flames but the desire is strong to involve Russia in a debilitating and prestige-destroying colonial war. Unfortunately America seems to have reached the point where the compulsion to act, however daft the action, is almost irresistible. Out-manœuvred in Africa, frustrated in Iran, the administration may yield to the temptation to try to score off Russia in Afghanistan. If they do so they will be repeating a historic mistake. It is difficult however, to see how such intervention could be achieved now that Pakistan has declined the offer of military aid and relations with Iran have been soured beyond sweetening. Ironically, the only other route would be through clandestine co-operation with the Chinese and it would not be entirely surprising if this had been one topic for discussion on US Defence Secretary Harold Brown's recent trip to Peking.

As for the other western nations, they must be even more impotent than the Americans. Lord Carrington's proposal to neutralize what had already been prior to the Russian invasion one of the most doggedly neutral countries in the third world, can only be an exploratory one. To suggest a UN guarantee is to express a touching belief in fairies, and great power guarantees invoke the apocalyptic spectres of recent history. The fact is that for a variety of reasons neither the western powers, nor the Islamic nations, nor Afghanistan's immediate neighbours are willing to help the guerrillas fight for the freedom whose loss those countries publicly so deplore. The only outside power, neighbouring or not, which can, short of a world war, determine what happens in Afghanistan, is Russia.

Russia's strategic aim in the region has undoubtedly been surreptitiously to create a state of chaos in which Pakistan would completely disintegrate, or at best shrivel to a relatively insignificant state consisting of only the Punjab and Sind, and to set up client states in Pushtunistan and Baluchistan as a result of revolutions nurtured through the agency of Afghan irredentism.

Amin's cry for help must, therefore, have rung most unpleasantly in Kremlin ears because it precipitated a situation Russia had been trying for twenty years to avoid — overt intervention in the government of Afghanistan. For Russia's gradualist policy to succeed it was necessary to have in Afghanistan a government so completely in thrall to the Soviet Union that it would have no option but to sponsor Soviet foreign policy. The Russians, however, had as completely misunderstood the spirit of Afghanistan as had the Americans and when Daoud began to reverse the centrist economic policy Russia favours, denounced Russian attempts at second-hand manipulation of the non-aligned states, and adopted a more conciliatory attitude over Pushtunistan, a Politburo flushed with recent successes elsewhere, precipitated a revolution that even with Soviet technical backing and advice the indigenous Communist Party was not powerful enough to see through.

The ferocity and fanaticism of reaction were quite underestimated by the Russians many of whom were, I think, quite genuinely shocked to find that they were not welcomed as liberators but execrated as invaders. Now, however, they are committed and have already incurred all the opprobrium forecast as the consequence of such an invasion. They have three choices. They can stay and fight; they can pull out Vietnam-style; or they can withdraw as part of a package.

There is no likelihood that they will make the second choice. Almost unassisted as they are, the freedom fighters cannot inflict unacceptable casualties on a country in which public opinion is both uninformed and unimportant. The loss of face involved in unconditional withdrawal would be even less acceptable to the Soviet Union than the loss of credibility entailed in the invasion.

The first choice in present circumstances has some attraction. A minor one is the opportunity it provides to blood and train Soviet forces. On the international scene it would clearly demonstrate to third world countries and especially to Iran, that Russia can and will use military force to achieve its aims with impunity and without western opposition in many parts of the world. Its threats become more real. As far as Afghanistan itself is concerned, President Karmal's régime would undoubtedly pursue policies which could in the long run increase its popularity, particularly among those sections of the community which have been the victims of religious and racial exploitation by the mullahs and the leading Pathan families; women, the racial minorities, and the debt-entangled poorer peasants. Its commitment to a drive for literacy must also broaden the base of its appeal in the long run.

The long run, however, usually proves a costly one and the Russian leadership knows it. The loss of western trade in grain and technology is damaging; the drain on the economy of sustaining such a large army in the field is even more so. Indeed, it is arguable that if undertaken for any great length of time it could lead to the collapse of the Soviet domestic economy and thus of the control of the ruling class. Moreover, Soviet ability to influence the third world diminishes with every day its forces remain in Afghanistan. Yet as long as the guerrillas fight Russia will have to stay, and many of them will fight for years. The only way for the Soviet army to achieve a decisive victory is by exterminating large sections of the Afghan population and emptying large tracts of the country of their inhabitants. Russia has, of course, both the ruthless will and means to do so, (though caution should be exercised in concluding from the presence of chemical warfare vehicles, equipment and ammunition that she intends to do so. It must be remembered that the Russian army is trained and equipped on the assumption that chemical warfare will be a normal constituent of future combat conditions). But would even limited genocide be expedient? As an alternative to military defeat, probably yes, but as an alternative to even a limited attainment of Russia's political objectives without military force, no. Clearly, as I view the Russian invasion as a reluctant recognition that Soviet foreign policy in Afghanistan was failing, I must believe the Russian claim that they would like to withdraw as soon as possible. Depending on how much help the rebels get, possible could be soon or never.

An attractive package could perhaps be put to various rebel leaders, though we have already noted the difficulty of negotiating with such an amorphous and uncoordinated movement. Participation in government, guarantees of religious freedom – it was noticeable that one of Karmal's first conciliatory acts was to remove the communist slogans from the streets of Kabul – elections in say two or three years time, commitment to pursue the Pushtunistan issue, and of course withdrawal of Russian troops as soon as peace is more or less restored, might just appeal to some rebel leaders. In exchange there would be required only a cessation of armed resistance to the government and a tacit endorsement of the Karmal régime. The more realistic rebel leaders know that they cannot drive the Russians out and for some at least the temptation to get back to the centre of power ahead of their tribal rivals might be great. The leaders of the Hazara, Tajik and Nuristani rebels might see such an agreement as a chance to redress the balance of power in their favour. Some leaders would undoubtedly refuse, some areas would continue to resist, but in all probability such rebellion would be no more extensive or disruptive than was found acceptable in the closing stages of Daoud's presidency and which might almost be regarded as endemic in Afghanistan. From the Russian point of view, the ideal relationship of the mid-70s would be restored and Russia could, once the world's indignation and feeble protests had evaported as they surely would, resume her quiet course of subversion in the region.

The only external factor which will influence the Russian choice is the effectiveness of rebel resistance. That effectiveness will depend on how much outside help they get — a fact which poses a considerable dilemma for the West in general and America in particular.

There are still substantial numbers of politicians in the West who believe that dialogue leading to detente should be a cardinal element in western relations with the Soviet Union. Dialogue between a man lying submissively on his back and one standing over him in hobnail boots tends to be rather one-sided. Those who recognize that Russia is in a high fever of imperalism which can only be checked by a *demonstration* of hard physical resistance are not necessarily fanatical cold warriors. There is no evidence since the war to suggest that the Soviet Union regards dialogue with the West as anything other than an opportunity to manoeuvre for practical advantage. A bloody check, such as would be inflicted by an unsuccessful campaign in Afghanistan, might make Soviet leaders recognize the need for genuine concessions and for genuine detente.

It would be difficult but not impossible for the West to find means of arming and supplying the Afghan freedom fighters to such an extent that they could severely embarrass the Soviet military, even if they had no hope of defeating them. But it would be Afghan lives, probably several hundred thousand of them, which would pay for that manoeuvre on the world stage. The dilemma is further compounded by the fact that to some extent freedom and reform appear to be on opposite sides. The history of Afghanistan throughout this century has been of reformers — Abdur Rahman, Amanullah, the 'democrats', even Daoud — being successfully defeated by the bigotry of the mullahs and the pugnacity of the Pathan tribes. The West, by encouraging the present rebellion, would be backing men whose policy if they were in unrestrained power would probably be an anathema to western liberal principles, in order to uphold the no less fundamental principle of a people's right to determine the pattern of their lives without external military interference. We are faced with a choice. Should we actively support the Afghan freedom fighters because in the bazaars of Kabul and Kandahar, in the mountains of Badakshan and the Hazarajat, in the tribal valleys of the south and the cities of the north, we feel that they are fighting the battle for *our* freedom, or should we recognize that the West's *prime* objective should be to further the interest of the Afghan people by securing the withdrawal of Russian troops? If the latter alternative is the right one we simply negate our diplomatic and public pressures on Russia, if we respond to our instincts and clandestinely support the freedom fighters. It might well be possible to secure a withdrawal of Russian troops if the freedom fighters as a whole could instead be persuaded to recognise the Karmal régime — tacitly at least. There remain two crucial questions. Would the great majority of the freedom fighters be prepared to give such recognition to the authority of the Karmal régime if they were given guarantees of religious freedom and some participation in government, and would the Russians run the risk of Karmal being no more able than his predecessors to hold power unaided by Soviet forces? If the answer to these two questions were yes, then I believe the West would be justified in any duplicity to gain the end, both in its own interest and that of the Afghans. A Karmal-Gailani coalition, for example, might well be made to serve western as well as Russian aims. Certainly it would be an acknowledgement of a fact that has been recognized for twenty years — namely that Afghanistan is basically within the sphere of Russian influence. But it would also achieve some social and economic reforms of which we could approve, probably exercise restraint in practice if not rhetoric over Pushtunistan, and most important of all reassert Afghan independence of foreign direction and intervention. It is on this innate Afghan spirit of independence that I believe the West should gamble. Past experience has shown that Afghan rulers of all shades of political opinion sooner or later demonstrate that they are above all nationalists who cherish their country's independence. Thus the 400 million dollars of US military aid rejected by Pakistan could be far more effectively spent in restoring the economic independence of a neutral Afghanistan. To ensure the genuineness of such neutrality the West should be prepared to go to considerable lengths. America, and by implication her western allies, should take up the Soviet challenge of a joint declaration of non-interference and a guarantee of Afghan neutrality. But let us also have the nerve to mean it, to make it appear that once they have withdrawn, early withdrawal being the *sine qua non* of agreement, if one Russian soldier or pilot crosses the Oxus again Afghanistan becomes the Poland of World War III. It is no exaggeration to say that if Afghanistan, Iran and Pakistan were to fall under the direct control of the Soviet

Union the balance of power might be tipped too far against the West to be recovered. The key to this region and the future of the subcontinent as a whole, is Afghanistan. The solution proposed is to put a great deal at hazard — but it could be the only chance of at least forcing a draw.

Epilogue – October 1980

Little has changed since the main text of this book was completed in June, except that with the Olympic propagandiad successfully concluded and world attention diverted by the oil-depriving war between Iran and Iraq, Soviet forces have been more easily able to step up the extent and ruthlessness of their onslaught on the Afghans. The freedom fighters still receive only a trickle of help from the outside world and that on the informal basis achieved by the personal machinations of the representatives of the various, still largely uncoordinated, guerrilla groups. Yet despite these difficulties they continue to put up a remarkably courageous and often effective resistance, not only in the countryside but in such major towns as Herat and Ghazni. They have become particularly adept at luring small Russian detachments into ambush and capturing the arms and ammunition with which to sustain their fight. Paradoxically there are some respects in which the effectiveness of the guerrillas suits Russian military leaders at least, even if it is unwelcome to the policy-makers in the

Kremlin. For the first time since World War II they have an opportunity to test men, weapons and organization in the kind of 'live' conditions the West, and indeed the Chinese, have experienced in Korea, Indo-China, Aden, Cyprus, the Oman, Northern Ireland and a dozen other places. The ruthlessness of the advantage they have been taking of that opportunity has become increasingly clear from guerrilla and military intelligence sources in recent months.

Once their invasion was complete, the initial Soviet approach was to use Afghan army and air force units to do most of the fighting, and to confine their own role to supplying moral and logistic support and occasionally bailing out the Afghan regulars when they got into trouble. By the end of April 1980, however, any pretence that the Russians were simply supporting the Afghan army had to be abandoned as unit after unit of the local forces went over to the freedom fighters until, by the late summer, no more than twenty thousand men of an army of almost one hundred thousand still responded to the orders from Kabul, and then without enthusiasm. Initially, too, the majority of air attacks were made by Soviet trained Afghan pilots. Now, the Afghan air force has been virtually grounded and many of its pilots have either been imprisoned or have deserted. The Russians, left without aircrew with local knowledge, have commandeered Afghan civil aircraft and impressed their crews, but now these too are deserting. The remaining Afghan army units have had all their heavy anti-tank and anti-aircraft weapons removed to prevent them falling, as they have done in some quantity, into the hands of the freedom fighters.

Apart from a few special KGB units, Soviet troops have had no training in counter-insurgency. This might be interpreted, after all, as an unacceptable, if tacit, admission of the unthinkable. The Soviet military assumption has been the classic one that their forces would be linking up with a co-operating Marxist fifth column in any field of likely operations, but this is conspicuously absent in Afghanistan. It is partly to offset the handicaps of their ignorance that the Russians have called in officers from their allies in South Yemen, Cuba and Vietnam. The Yemenis are used to fighting in terrain very similar to that of Afghanistan, the Cubans have undertaken counter-insurgency operations in Angola, and the Vietnamese, the most combat-experienced troops in the world, are also the masters of how to give logistic support to large bodies of men operating in difficult and hostile country.

The Russians want their own men to acquire this experience. The initial invasion force of just under one hundred thousand men constituted less than one-seventeenth of Soviet ready forces, and Brezhnev's much trumpeted pre-Olympic withdrawal was no more than a normal rotation of conscript troops designed to sustain morale, to give combat experience to as many men as possible, and to replace irrelevant equipment. This rotation has been on an individual rather than a unit basis in accordance with usual Soviet practice, and by this means as many as a quarter of a million men may have served in Afghanistan by the end of 1980. In the ordinary divisions, only officers and sergeants will have had lengthy exposure to the Afghan campaign and conversely, in the two Airborne Divisions, while rotation of troops is slower, commanders from the other five Airborne Divisions are being brought in for training; so, too, are the crews of helicopter gunships based in Russia and East Germany.

It is apparent from their conduct of the campaign that Russia's generals have also been learning tactics and techniques from the West. For example, though the response to a guerrilla ambush is often an airstrike of limited effectiveness in such terrain, with increasing frequency the Russians are taking a leaf out of the Rhodesian security forces' book, dropping crack airborne troops between the guerrillas and their bases, while a second parachute unit acts as beaters.

Following US experience in Vietnam, the Russians seem to be trying to create Free Fire Zones round the major cities, particularly Kabul. The population of adjacent villages for fifteen to twenty miles around is being driven out and the villages razed. Thereafter anything that moves in the zone without authority is blasted out of existence. The fire power deployed by the Soviet divisions is enormous. Each has, for example, eighteen BM 21 rocket launchers, each with forty tubes and capable of putting down eight tons of high explosive in thirty seconds and reloading within ten minutes.

A variety of weapons are used against guerrillas on the ground, ranging from cluster bombs (the effect is like scattering huge bags of grenades) to the AGS 30mm 30-round grenade launcher, whose accurate range is 1500 metres – ironically a weapon closely based on an American designed one never produced in the West. By far the deadliest weapon in the Soviet army in Afghanistan is the world's most lethal helicopter gunship, the Hinde D. This is armed with four rocket pods, each with thirty-two 57mm rockets, a laser-sighted 12.7mm rotary cannon firing a thousand rounds a minute, and either four anti-tank missiles or four 500 kg napalm or HE bombs. Not surprisingly, a Hinde D is capable of annihilating an entire village in a few seconds with scarcely any exposure of itself to ground fire. In any case, the three-man crew in its titanium bullet-proof cockpits are well-protected – though the six assault troops that can be carried aft are more vulnerable.

For the time being the Russians are still learning and still make mistakes, but they seem quite prepared to settle down for a long struggle as they dig themselves into concrete bases like the one at Bagram (only an hour's flight from the Strait of Hormuz). How the struggle will go when the Russians have gained more experience is anyone's guess, but unless the freedom fighters get more help than they are receiving now, the odds against them increase daily. They are not improved by the massive disruption the fighting has caused to the normal pattern of agriculture. This has not just been in the sowing and harvesting of grain and fruit crops, but in the movement of herds to their various seasonal pastures. The Soviet forces used the immobility imposed on the guerrillas by the snows of their first post-invasion winter, to consolidate their bases and communications and to await the spring offensive of the freedom fighters. These, in turn, used that season to build up their strength and organize, albeit often on the Pakistan side of the border. This winter as the Russians sit tight in their cantonments and concrete bunkers, they will know that starvation is thinning the ranks and sapping the morale of their enemy — for the whole non-subservient Afghan population is now seen as such. When Afghanistan last suffered a famine in the early 70s large imports of American grain saved the day. President Karmal could scarcely permit such a rescue again, even if it were offered. The Russians, themselves likely to be in difficulties without US grain imports, can scarcely fill the gap, though no doubt they will try to use the opportunity to buy loyalty with bread if they can. They may no longer be surprised to find that there will not be many genuine takers. Without a major injection of outside help the Afghan freedom fighters must find themselves weaker in the second spring of their resistance than during the first, in which they inflicted so many, if individually limited, reverses on government forces and, latterly, on the Russian invaders themselves.

The best use to which the West can put the winter months is to help engineer the conditions, however specious, and however apparent the concessions yielded, in which a compromise government can be set up and the Russians enabled gradually to withdraw. Once they are gone they can then be kept out — at a price.

References

Chapter 1

1. Nancy Dupree, *Afghanistan*. Kabul: Afghan Tourist Organization, 1971.
2. Nancy Dupree, *op. cit.*
3. Sir W. Fraser-Tytler, *Afghanistan*. London and New York: Oxford University Press, 2nd Edition 1953, p. 28.
4. *Baburnama*, p. 136.
5. *Ibid*, p. 138.
6. Cited in Fraser-Tytler, *op. cit.*, p. 50.
7. Mountstuart Elphinstone, *Account of the Kingdom of Caubul*. London: 1815.

Chapter 2

1. John McNeill to Lord Palmerston, 11 April 1838. *Correspondence Relating to Persia and Afghanistan*. Printed for Her Majesty's Government by J. Harrison and Son, London, 1839. Cited in Fraser-Tytler, *op. cit.*, p. 100.
2. Cited in Fraser-Tytler, *op. cit.*, p. 319.
3. Cited in Nancy Dupree, *op. cit.*
4. Sir Thomas Holdich, *The Indian Borderland*. London: Methuen, 1901, pp. 366, 371.
5. Cited in Fraser-Tytler, *op. cit.*, p. 319.
6. Cited in Fraser-Tytler, *op. cit.*, p. 138.
7. Cited in John Morley, *Life of Gladstone*. London: Macmillan, 1906 Edition, Vol. 11, p. 203.
8. Cited in Fraser-Tytler, *op. cit.*, p. 153.
9. Holdich, *op. cit.*, p. 50.

10. Cited in R. I. Bruce, *The Forward Policy and its Results.* London: 1900, p. 347.

11. Hansard, House of Lords Debates, 7 March 1898.

12. *Memoirs of Count Pahlen* (trans. N.J. Couriss). London and New York: Oxford University Press, 1964.

13. A. Baker, *Wings Over Kabul.* London: William Kimber, 1975.

Chapter 3

1. James Thomson. *The Seasons: 'Summer'.* 1727 Edition.

2. *The Pakhtun Question.* Pamphlet. Afghanistan Government, 1956.

3. *Ibid.*

4. Elphinstone, *op. cit.,* p. 253.

Chapter 4

1. Louis Dupree, *Afghanistan.* Princeton: Princeton University Press, 1973.

Chapter 6

1. R. T. Akhramovich, *Outline History of Afghanistan After the Second World War.* Moscow: 1966.

2. *Ibid.*

3. Louis Dupree, *op. cit.*

4. Nake Kamrany, *Peaceful Competition in Afghanistan.* Washington: 1968.

5. Akhramovich, *op. cit.*

6. Louis Dupree, *op. cit.*

7. Akhramovich, *op. cit.*

8. Kamrany, *op. cit.*

Chapter 9

1. Cited in Louis Dupree, *op. cit.*

Index

Consistency of nomenclature and spelling is not easy in the Afghan context. For spelling I use that given me by the person himself, my informant or the main written source. Thus 'Mohammed' may be spelt 'Mohammad', 'Muhammad', etc. In cases of countries important in the Afghan context which have changed name during our period, i.e. Persia/Iran, Russia/Soviet Union, I have used that pertaining to the time referred to, but cross reference is prudent. Where the association is of relatively minor importance, I list people, country, adjective, etc, under the country, thus 'Germany' covers 'German, Germans, Germany and West Germany'.

I should also note that while I personally think of them as 'freedom fighters', these courageous patriots are also indexed separately as 'guerrillas' where their military role is referred to and as 'rebels' when the point of view is that of the Russians or the Afghan Government. Entries for 'taxation', 'exports', etc, will be found under 'economy', those for 'cotton', 'land ownership', etc, under 'agriculture' and so on. Place name references in the text are indexed only when the location is significant or conveys the nature of the place mentioned.